Growing Vegetables in the Great Plains

Growing Vegetables in the Great Plains

Joseph R. Thomasson

Illustrations by Martin B. Capron

 **University Press of Kansas**

Cover and interior design by John Baxter

Published by the University Press of Kansas (Lawrence, Kansas 66045), which was organized by the Kansas Board of Regents and is operated and funded by Emporia State University, Fort Hays State University, Kansas State University, Pittsburg State University, the University of Kansas, and Wichita State University

Library of Congress Cataloging-in-Publication Data
Thomasson, Joseph R.
    Growing Vegetables in the Great Plains / Joseph R. Thomasson
        p. cm.
    Includes bibliographical references and index.
    ISBN 0-7006-0429-4 (cloth)   — ISBN 0-7006-0430-8 (pbk.)

    1. Vegetable gardening—Great Plains.   I. Title.
SB321.T42 1990
635'.0978—dc20   90-12440
                                                  CIP

Printed in the United States of America
10 9 8 7 6 5 4 3 2 1

To Nadine, Russ, Heather, and Scotty,
    my favorite garden companions,
and to my father and mother, Aunt Louise,
and Felix and Florine,
    who made many things possible

Contents

Preface ix

Chapter 1 **Getting Started** 1
A Beginning — Learning about Gardening 1
Thomasson's Rules for Choosing a Garden Spot 1
Preparing the Garden Spot 3
Selecting Vegetables and Vegetable Varieties for Your Garden 5
Did You Know? Soils 6

Chapter 2 **Growing Your Own Transplants** 10
The Advantages of Growing Transplants 10
The Economics of Growing Transplants 11
How to Grow Transplants 12
Into the Real World: Transplanting Your Plants 16

Chapter 3 **Plant Nutrition** 18
Using Fertilizers 18
Soil pH 20

Chapter 4 **Mulches** 22

Chapter 5 **Pest and Disease Control** 25
Consider Your Options 25
Know Your Enemies and Your Friends 27
Beneficial Insects in the Garden 28
Pesticide Safety 29
Did You Know? Insect Structures and Patterns 30
Products I Use in My Vegetable Garden 33
A Special Grasshopper Cocktail 35
Common Synthetic Pesticides 35
The Really Big Pests 38

Chapter 6 **Weeds** 44
What Is a Weed Anyway? 44
Achieving Cheap, Permanent Weed Control 44
If the Disturbance-Timing Method Doesn't Work 46

Chapter 7 **Managing Water in Great Plains Gardens** 47

Chapter 8 **Gardening in the Wind** 50
Protecting Your Garden from the Wind 51

Chapter 9   **Is There Garden Life after a Hailstorm?** 54

Chapter 10   **The Farmers' Market: Sharing the Bounty** 59

Chapter 11   **Vegetable Lineup** 61

Asparagus 61

Beans 64

Beets 67

Did You Know? Plant Hairs 68

Broccoli, Brussels Sprouts, Cabbage, and Cauliflower 70

Cantaloupe and Watermelons 77

Carrots 79

Did You Know? Pollen 80

Celery, Dill, and Parsley 83

Corn 84

Cucumbers 87

Eggplants 90

Did You Know? Insects and Pollination 92

Huckleberries 94

Leafy Greens: Lettuce, Spinach, and Swiss Chard 95

Okra 99

The Onion Family: Onions, Chives, Garlic, and Shallots 100

Did You Know? Stinging Insects 102

Peanuts 103

Peas 104

Peppers 106

Potatoes 108

Pumpkins 111

Radishes 112

Did You Know? Stomata and Transpiration 113

Rhubarb 115

Squash 117

Strawberries 120

Did You Know? Transport Systems 122

Sweet Potatoes 124

Tomatoes 126

Appendixes   1 My Favorite Recipes 131

2 Flower Varieties to Plant near Heartland Vegetable Gardens 137

Annotated Bibliography 139

Index 141

Preface

I am a scientist and teacher by training (presently at Fort Hays State University, Hays, Kansas) and a gardener by hobby, and I love being all three. As a teacher whose professional training is in the study of plants, or botany, I enjoy interacting and sharing information about plants with anyone who will listen. As a gardener and scientist, I enjoy watching plants grow and experimenting in my garden with different varieties of vegetable and fruit plants and with the conditions that affect their development. This book is an outgrowth of my interests and experiments in my gardens in central Iowa, west-central Kansas, the northern Black Hills of South Dakota, the eastern slope of the Rocky Mountains in Colorado, and southwestern Texas during the last seventeen years.

It may appear unnecessary to publish one more gardening book when there are so many already on the market. It would seem that whether one is an expert or a beginning gardener, enough information already is available on every aspect of gardening, be it wide row or square foot, standard or raised, organic or hydroponic. However, I consider my book sufficiently different from others that it will be a valuable new source of information to beginning and veteran vegetable gardeners. It is especially directed toward gardening in the Heartland, or Great Plains, of the United States, an area stretching from North Dakota south to Texas and from the foothills of the Rocky Mountains in Colorado east to western Iowa and Missouri. The Heartland as described herein is characterized predominantly by prairies and plains, but it also includes adjacent areas to the west such as the foothills of the Rocky Mountains and the Black Hills in South Dakota and the margins of the deciduous woods to the east. (I use "Heartland" and "Great Plains" interchangeably throughout the book.)

Not only do I share practical information about such aspects of gardening as growing techniques, productive and disease-resistant plant varieties, and the pests and diseases most likely attack your garden, but also I provide a look at the marvelous structure of the soil, plants, and insects found in the garden through the use of a scanning electron microscope (SEM). This instrument is capable of magnifying objects in three dimensions as high as 500,000 times.

During my years of gardening in the central United States, I have become aware, sometimes painfully so, that environmental conditions in this region are often quite different from those in Rhode Island and Washington, where I lived for short periods. Gardening procedures must be adjusted accordingly, and currently available gardening books do not always cover these adjustments sufficiently. For example, two recently published, excellent, and beautifully illustrated gardening books that I have on my shelf, and that should be on every gardener's shelf, were obviously compiled without sufficient experience from gardeners in the central United States. How do I know? Because the word "wind" does not even appear in the index of one, and the problem of wind is mentioned only briefly in the text of both. Hail, another dreaded factor in many areas of the Great Plains, is discussed in neither.

The Heartland gardener has to understand the region's special conditions early or face frustration and disappointment in the garden. Thus one of the goals of my book is to provide information I hope will help you to deal more successfully with these differences. Similarly, although some of the diseases and pests found in other regions of the country are also found in the central United States, others are not or are more or less common in this area. I hope to alert you to what will probably attack your vegetables in this region. Finally, I have found that some varieties of vegetables have worked exceptionally well in the Great Plains while others have failed badly, and following a discussion of each vegetable, I have included a description of the many varieties I have tried, as well as which varieties are my favorites. I would emphasize that the varieties I list are only suggestions that can be used as a starting point. I encourage you to experiment with varieties until you find those that work best for you. I have presented much of the "how to" instructions for growing vegetables in individual sections in numbered steps. Although veteran gardeners may find some of this information repetitive, I am assuming that some readers have never planted a garden. I hope all of this information will help you to have as much fun and success as I have had gardening.

As a gardener, I am especially interested in the practical knowledge I gain by growing plants and in the produce I can harvest and eat. However, as a botanist, I find plants and their complexity extremely exciting and stimulating, and the beauty of structures found in plants as well as associated insects and soil in the garden is unmatched. I am delighted to be able to share this beauty with you through a series of "Did You Know?" sections throughout the book. I also present practical information about gardening in these sections. All of the pictures were taken by me with a scanning electron microscope, and, with rare exception, all of the insects and materials in these photographs were gathered from my gardens. The "inner space" of the garden is truly a world of wonders!

Throughout I give recommendations for the control of pests and diseases in the garden. Mostly I recommend the use of natural products such as insecticidal soaps and the pesticides pyrethrum and rotenone, but I would caution you that even though these are relatively nontoxic to humans, you should still be careful when you use them. I avoid the use of most synthetic poisons because their effects on humans and the environment are simply not documented well enough for me, and I choose not to expose my family to them. Assurances by "experts" that they are safe do not reassure me either. Not long ago chlordane, sold as a 10 percent dust and recommended for pest and weed control in vegetable gardens and lawns, was shown to cause serious health problems, and Kelthane, widely recommended as a miticide in vegetable gardens, is under review by the Environmental Protection Agency.

One of the most interesting aspects of gardening is its history. Methods of gardening have been recorded for many centuries, and in some cases the methods we currently use are little changed from those used, say, in the Middle Ages. In various sections of my book, I include quotations about vegetables and gardening from a medieval medicinal herbal published in 1633 by John Gerard called *The Herball or Generall Historie of Plantes*. The quotations, which I have left in the original Old English, provide some intriguing information about seventeenth-century gardeners and their vegetables and suggest that many things we enjoy about gardening transcend time.

Chapter 9 — "Is there Garden Life after a Hailstorm?" — originally appeared as "Hailstorm!" in the August 1985 issue of *Gardens for All* (now *National Gardening Magazine*). Some of the color photographs were made possible through a contribution from TerraCopia, Inc. A portion of the proceeds from the sale of this book are being donated to the children's gardening programs of the National Gardening Association, Burlington, Vermont.

I am indebted to many gardening friends I have known over the years for sharing their excitement and ideas about gardening with me. I have also learned from them that gardening, like any endeavor in life, is a continual learning process. With this in mind, I would encourage you to let me know about your successes (or failures, which I hope are few) with my methods, recommended varieties, and so on. Gardening is without doubt one of the most rewarding, relaxing, and healthy activities in which anyone, of any age, can participate; perhaps that is why so many people garden. I am confident that reading my book will help you enjoy gardening even more!

Joseph R. Thomasson
Hays, Kansas

Growing Vegetables
in the Great Plains

Chapter One Getting Started

**A Beginning —
Learning about
Gardening**

There are two major ways to learn about gardening — by doing it and reading about it. By doing, you learn firsthand the many aspects of gardening, including what techniques or varieties work best and what insects attack particular crops. Although learning by doing (or experience) is probably the most fun, the disadvantage is that it can sometimes take several years to gather the necessary data about the desirability of using a particular variety, technique, and so on. This is where reading fills the gap. By reading, you can reap the benefit of the knowledge acquired by other gardeners from many years of experience. Even though some of that information might not be useful to you, most of it will, and no matter how many years you've gardened or how much you know about plants, there's always more to learn. That, in fact, is what makes gardening so exciting and challenging!

Reading materials are available on every aspect of gardening and range from county or state agency bulletins to magazines and books for sale by private publishers. Most of these are fine sources of information on gardening, and I have listed a few in the bibliography. Let me stress that there are many other valuable publications on gardening in addition to these, but my list should give you a good start. Visit or contact a bookstore or your local or state agricultural extension offices for more information on gardening publications.

**Thomasson's
Rules for Choosing
a Garden Spot**

Now that you've decided to garden, you'll first need to select a garden spot. If you've gardened previously, you're probably familiar with most of the information in this section and might be tempted to skip it. However, if you're like I am, every review helps, and I'd encourage you to at least skim the information. If you've never gardened before, you're in luck, because I've written this section with the beginner in mind.
¶ Relax. Realize that the perfect garden spot does not exist, except perhaps on TV gardening programs, and even those I doubt! Your

garden's location is going to be a compromise among all of the situations that exist where you live. Some, such as the amount of organic matter in the soil, you can change readily; others such as the weather, you can't. Keep foremost in mind that gardening should give you a lot of pleasure; plan the location of your garden spot accordingly.

¶ Locate in the sun. Your plot must be in the sun for the majority of vegetables to thrive. Otherwise, you will be in for spindly plants stretching toward what sun they can get for photosynthesis to make sugars for growth and respiration. Such plants will expend very little energy in producing fruit. Situate your garden where it will receive at least 6 to 8 hours of direct, uninterrupted sunlight. Don't settle for bright shade, because tomatoes will be leggy with few fruits, and radishes will be all tops. Try to determine the pattern of light over your garden spot during the growing season so your plot and its soil is exposed to lots of sunlight. This may be especially important in the early spring and late fall if

you want to use the warmth from the sun to help prevent frost damage as much as possible.

¶ Determine the drainage. Learn how the water drains from the area you intend to garden. Plan the garden location so that there are no low spots where the water collects and stands for long periods of time. Don't worry about water standing for 1 or 2 hours; as long as it drains away in a reasonable length of time, you can garden there. I've gardened on a plot that occasionally was almost completely under water after a 2- to 3-inch rain, but it caused no permanent problems. Be sure that the garden is not in the path of heavy drainage in the case of torrential rains, or your garden and plants may be washed away.

¶ Watch the wind. Many areas in the Great Plains are very windy during at least part of the growing season. When the wind blows, try to see which parts of your garden are most severely affected so that you can plan accordingly when you plant your vegetables. You may even want to construct a fence or plant a perennial windbreak (for example, asparagus) to break wind-flow patterns.

¶ Consider the view. If possible, locate your garden so you can enjoy watching it grow — outside the bedroom window, outside the kitchen window, or outside a set of sliding glass doors. It's always amazing how much you learn (how fast corn grows, how a robin searches for grubs, and so on), and how relaxing it is, except when it hails.

Preparing the Garden Spot

Preparing your garden spot is as important as its location, because this is where your plants will literally have their feet, or roots, in the soil. If I were to stress any advice, it would be not to skimp on this aspect of gardening.

¶ Consider timing. If at all possible plan your garden so that the first soil preparation is done in the fall. This allows nature to work on the soil the entire winter through freezing and thawing and the action of micro-organisms. It is remarkable how soft even the hardest of clay soils can become over a single winter season.

¶ Identify and decide what to do with the original plant cover. Examine the type of plants covering the future garden site. If they are annuals such as foxtail grasses or sunflowers, you can mow or burn the area to reduce the number of seeds that will remain in your plot; if these seeds germinate, the plants you see will be weeds. Bunch grasses such as fescue and rye can be left in place with no further treatment until the next step. If you have a severe infestation of a perennial weed such as bindweed, or if you are starting with an area covered by a plant like bermuda grass, you may want to kill them either by covering the plot

3

with black plastic during the summer (this works well on small plots) or by using a chemical plant killer such as Roundup. If you do nothing, these weeds will be a constant source of agony, in the form of backaches and so on, for several years.

¶ Till the plot. Thoroughly till the soil to a depth of at least 12 inches either by hand digging or with a power tiller. If the original plant cover consisted of noninvasive plants, such as fescue or annual rye, turn them into the soil to provide extra organic matter. If you use a tiller, get a sturdy 7- or 8-horsepower model (for example, Troy-Bilt). You will probably have to turn the soil several times in order to loosen it deeply enough, especially if the site was formerly a lawn.

¶ Have a soil test done. Although this step is not essential, it will eliminate much guesswork on your part. Your local county extension office can tell you how to have a soil test done on your plot, usually for less than $10. This test will give you an idea of how much organic matter, fertilizer, and so on, you should add to the soil.

¶ Add organic matter. Unless you are exceedingly lucky, you'll undoubtedly have to add organic matter to make your soil "soft" and workable. The exact amount will depend on your original soil conditions, but your goal is to have a soil that is crumbly and loose. In Colorado and Texas, I started with very sandy substrates, whereas in Kansas, I started with a heavy clay base. These situations were frustrating at first, but by adding abundant organic matter, I was able to modify both the sandy and the clay bases into excellent gardening soils. As sources of organic matter, I highly recommend baled peat moss, herbicide- and pesticide-free grass clippings, clean wheat straw, leaves gathered in the fall, or compost. The amount you apply will depend on your situation; generally it varies from 3 to 6 inches deep before tilling. If you use leaves, do not use black walnut, because these contain substances that can actually prevent your seeds from germinating in the spring. Manure can be a wonderful addition to any soil, but unless you know the exact source and contents, I do not recommend its use. First, manure can be a source of perennial weeds, such as bindweed; second, some chemical insecticides and antibiotics fed to livestock find their way into the animals' wastes. When you buy packaged manures, you frequently have no idea of their origin or what is in them. If you read the labels, they sometimes contain a disclaimer of responsibility for their use!

¶ Add fertilizers and other materials. Add fertilizers as indicated by your soil test or as suggested in my book under "Growing Essentials" for a particular vegetable. Depending on the nature of your soil, you may also have to add other materials — for example, gypsum, to loosen clay and neutralize sodium salts; aluminum sulphate or organic matter to make your soil more acidic; or lime, to make your soil more alkaline. Add these materials only after you understand the basic nature of your soil, or they may produce undesirable effects. For example, adding gypsum to an already calcium-rich soil (typical of many Great Plains soils) will only create an undesirable situation of increased calcium salts in the soil. Always read and follow any warnings on boxes or sacks of fertilizer or other materials.

¶ Consider raised beds. If your soil is not well drained, you may want to consider making raised beds. Simply mark off your garden into smaller areas and surround them with pine (not permanent but less expensive) or redwood or cedar (relatively permanent but expensive) 2 × 4s or 2 × 6s, or with cinder blocks (expensive but permanent). Dig the walkways about 2 inches deep and put the soil in the raised beds. If desired, cover the walkways with grass or straw so that they will be passable after rains. The advantages of raised beds over other beds are that they drain better and warm up more quickly in the spring. The disadvantages are that they cost a lot to construct, although you can sometimes find free materials at a local city dump; they create problems in working the soil (for example, each bed must be tilled separately); and they dessicate more rapidly than other beds during hot weather (an important consideration in windy areas).

¶ Till once in the fall and once (maybe) in the spring. Each year following the first hard frost that kills your plants, remove the debris from your garden. Then spread organic matter (for example, leaves, peat moss, or straw) and any other desired materials (for example, gypsum) on your garden and till them in thoroughly. In the spring, after the soil has dried sufficiently, you may need to work your soil once again to loosen it for planting. If you can dig easily with your hand 6 or 8 inches into the soil, I wouldn't till; if you can't, till through it only once. Avoid any temptation to work it more than once ("just one more time to make it finer"), because if you work it too much, you'll probably create conditions that will pack your soil and make it a good source for bricks. If it rains after you work it but before you can plant, don't worry; you'll find that after it drains adequately, the soil will be nice and soft for planting.

Selecting Vegetables and Vegetable Varieties for Your Garden

At his home on the edge of the Black Hills in South Dakota, a friend remarked to me how poorly his tomatoes were doing. He assured me that he had done nothing different from the previous year when he had raised a bumper crop. His plants were not diseased and the weather had

Did You Know?

Soils

The Beautiful

The world below the surface of your garden is a mixture of particles that includes sand, silt, clay, and organic matter. The relations among these particles are complex and determine such soil characteristics as texture and drainage. The ability of a plant to survive and thrive is in many ways dependent on the correct balance of the particles with one another and with the living organisms in the soil. When viewed at the microscopic level, few subjects for exploration are as beautiful as soil components.

Clay, silt, and sand, the inorganic particles of the soil, are generally identified by their size and shape. Sand particles are usually visible to the naked eye and grade into smaller particles called silt. Sand and silt particles may be rounded to very irregular in shape. Clay particles are much smaller than either sand or silt, flat, and frequently stacked together like playing cards. I often try to relate the sizes of inorganic soil particles to gardeners by comparing sands and silts to pumpkins and tomatoes, and clays to pepper seeds.

The organic matter component of the soil is developed from parts of decaying organisms. One action of this organic matter in the soil is to separate smaller inorganic soil particles, such as silts and clays, so that water, minerals, and roots can penetrate the soil. With the larger sand particles, the organic matter fills the spaces between the particles and slows the loss of water and minerals by drainage. In a clay soil, any pores that might be present would be very small. Such a soil would be described as "tight." On the other hand, a sandy soil consists of much larger particles with spaces between the particles. The photographs on pages 6–7 show the intricate structure and remarkable relations of various soil components.

The Practical

¶ Soils that are clay rich will be "tight" since the clay particles will have little if any space between them. Water, minerals, and plant roots will have difficulty penetrating such soils. These soils compact easily, have poor drainage, and crack badly when dry. Adding sand and organic matter to such soils opens up and softens them, making them better for plant growth.

¶ Soils that are too sandy will be loose and often mineral poor since the voids between the larger sand particles permit rapid drainage of water and minerals. Such soils dry out rapidly after watering, and plants growing in them wilt quickly. Adding organic matter to sandy soils will slow drainage through them and increase their water- and mineral-holding capacity.

¶ Adding organic matter or fertilizers to any soil may change its acidity or alkalinity. Be sure to consider the effects on the soil of adding such materials when preparing your garden plot (see the section on soil pH in chapter 3).

Clay soils are sometimes referred to as being "tight" or "heavy." This is because the particles making up clay are tiny and frequently packed closely together. The surface of clay (top, magnified 15 times) shows no obvious pore spaces, and upon considerable magnification (bottom, magnified 2,600 times), clay particles can be seen stacked closely together like playing cards. Little wonder that water, minerals, and roots have a difficult time penetrating into soils with a high clay content. The addition of sand and organic particles to such soils helps to improve the tilth of the soil and makes it more suitable for the growth and spread of roots.

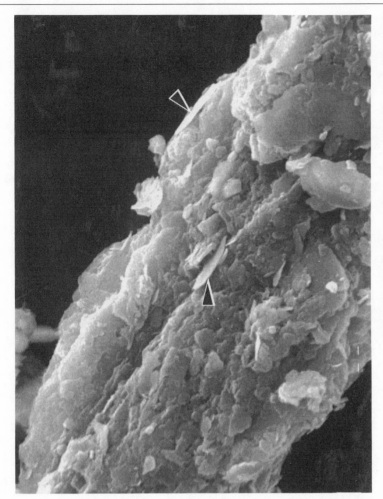

Sandy soils lacking organic matter (top right, magnified 15 times) contain large, empty air spaces between sand grains that allow water and minerals to pass through rapidly. As a result, such soils dry out quickly and require frequent applications of fertilizer.

A sandy soil (bottom right, magnified 15 times) with organic matter (at arrows) will have the ability to soak up and hold moisture and mineral nutri-ents. Roots penetrating such soils will be able to more easily locate and ab-sorb water and minerals, and plants will be less likely to wilt.

Clay particles (above left at arrows; magnified 2,800 times) that serve to retain minerals in the soil are shown combined with a piece of organic mat-ter. Associations of sand grains, clay particles, and organic matter form a fertile, easily worked soil.

not varied significantly from the previous year, so he was at a loss to explain why his tomatoes were not producing well. As we examined his plants, I asked him what variety they were. He didn't know. When I asked him what variety he planted the year before, he wasn't sure. Aware of my avid gardening nature (he is a remarkable professor of special education) he explained apologetically that "I always buy whatever is available at the store, maybe Sioux or something like that." Since there was no other explanation, I concluded that the difference he was experiencing in the vigor and production of his plants was probably due to a change in varieties from one year to the next.

My friend was guilty of one of the most common mistakes that many beginning and some longtime gardeners make: believing that any vegetable variety, if treated properly, will grow and produce well any-where. The fact is there are striking differences in how a variety of vegetable will perform under different environmental conditions. There is abundant evidence, for example, that shows that many vegetable varieties which do well in North Carolina fail miserably in Kansas or Colorado. Usually the most successful gardeners have learned this early in their gardening careers, and they pay careful attention to the selection of vegetable varieties as they plan their garden. The following tips should help you choose the vegetables and varieties that are best for your garden.

¶ Draw a garden map and make plans. Draw a map of your planned garden and outline which areas will be used for each vegetable. Decide which vegetables your family likes to eat, and how many varieties of each you want to plant. Allow spacing between plants and rows as indicated on the seed packages or as I have indicated in this book under particular vegetables. Then estimate how many seeds and transplants you'll need. Don't worry about underestimating what you'll need; I've never known a gardener who didn't have boxes or drawers full of seeds from previous years (we all swear we ordered just the amount we would use)!

¶ Plan for succession planting. After your cool-season vegetables (for example, broccoli and lettuce) have been harvested, you can plant many warm-season vegetables (for example, beans, corn, and squash) in the same location. This is called succession planting and will allow you to make maximum use of your garden space. Pay careful attention to days to maturity when selecting vegetable varieties for succession planting since shorter-maturing types may be needed to ensure that both the first and second crops will produce fruit in a single season in your area.

¶ Talk to local gardeners. Ask gardeners in your area which varieties they have had the best luck in growing. Be sure to ask them if they give any special treatment to their plants.

¶ Visit with your local extension agent. Most extension agents, especially if they have been in a region for some time, are quite knowledgeable about which varieties do best in a particular area. They can also alert you to varieties that are likely to be resistant to diseases common to your area.

¶ Consult recommended varieties lists. Most state agricultural universities have developed lists of recommended varieties for a state. You can obtain a list either from your local extension agent or from a university agriculture department. Keep in mind that these lists are usually very conservative — simply because a vegetable or a variety is not on the list does not mean you can't grow it. For example, the current Kansas list does not recommend planting head lettuce in the spring, yet I always raise excellent crops in the spring in west-central Kansas.

¶ Use All-American Selection (AAS) varieties. These are vegetable varieties (for example, Autumn Gold pumpkin and Sugar Snap peas) that have been tested and found excellent for home gardens by the nonprofit organization All-America Selections. Most seed catalogs prominently feature and recommend AAS varieties.

¶ Experiment. Don't be afraid to try new vegetables and varieties. I like to give newcomers at least a couple of years in my garden to prove themselves.

¶ Keep records. Write down the names of the varieties you use, when and how you planted them, and how they performed. There is nothing more frustrating than having great success with a vegetable variety and then not remembering its name. Records don't need to be elaborate or detailed so long as they serve your needs.

Chapter Two # Growing Your Own Transplants

The Advantages of Growing Transplants

In many areas, including the Great Plains, it is simply not practical to grow many types of plants in the garden directly from seed. The vegetables I am of course referring to are ones that most gardeners purchase as transplants — tomatoes, peppers, eggplants, broccoli, and so on. But have you ever considered growing your own seedlings for transplanting? Not only is it easy, but there are several other advantages. First, growing your own transplants allows the planting urge, a characteristic of every gardener, to begin to escape after several months of confinement by ice, snow, and cold. We all know the excitement those brightly colored seed catalogs cause when they arrive in late winter. Looking at the pictures, you can easily envision many varieties of vegetables lush and full of fruit in your garden. But then you remember that the garden is still several months away. By growing your own transplants, however, you can start to watch your garden grow 6 to 12 weeks before it even gets outside. For me, it is almost as exciting to see the first celery or tomato seedling push through the surface of the starting mix as it is to pick the first ripe tomato!

Second, you, the gardener, are allowed to select the varieties you want to plant. When you buy transplants locally, you are always limited to varieties that stores or greenhouses have available. When you start plants from seeds and grow them yourself, you decide what you will grow. Of course, if you are as optimistic and as excited as I am at this point in late winter, you'll probably buy more seeds than you could possibly use in 5 gardens! I always rationalize this excess by reminding myself that I'm supporting a job somewhere. Third, you may avoid bringing unwelcome diseases into your garden. Tomato plants, for example, are very susceptible to tobacco mosaic virus, an untreatable disease that greatly reduces vitality and production. This disease can be spread through virally infected tobacco found in cigarettes, and if smokers in the greenhouse or store where you buy gardening supplies touch transplants, they may inadvertently and unknowingly transmit the virus to the plants. You end up with diseased plants and poor production.

Fourth, growing your own transplants is relatively inexpensive. For a 20- by-50-foot garden, the total cost, not including the seeds, should be under $35. Seeds, depending on how many varieties you want to plant, will cost $10 to $30. Keep in mind that the most expensive items, such as fluorescent lamps, will last for many years and some of the seeds (for example, tomatoes) may be used for 2 to 3 years. Fifth, you can plan for the transplants when you want them. One of the problems I encountered in both Kansas and South Dakota was that young plants of the correct age for cool season crops (for example, broccoli) were usually not available when they should have been transplanted. By growing your own plants, you eliminate this uncertainty. I, for instance, like to use devices such as Wallo'Waters to see if I can have extra-early, vine-ripened tomatoes. Growing your own plants assures you that transplants will be available for these experiments.

Sixth, you can help your neighbors, friends, and relatives. I always grow a few extra transplants to give away. Other gardeners always appreciate receiving them, and knowing that one of the plants you "gave birth to" is encouraging the gardening urge in someone is a good feeling. Besides, stopping by later to visit one of your transplant offspring is another good excuse to talk gardening. Finally, if you have young children or grandchildren, it is an easy way to share a little time and the excitement of gardening with them. The additional questions you'll have to answer will mean taking a little longer to complete the planting, but you'll all remember those cold winter days as having had a little more warmth.

The Economics of Growing Transplants

In the long run, growing your own transplants does not have to be expensive. Here are the materials you need to grow enough transplants for a 20-by-50-foot garden plot:

Cost of Supplies (less $10 to $30 for seeds)
2 fluorescent lamps $20.00
4 starting flats and trays 6.00

8 quarts of starting mix 6.00
Water-soluble fertilizer 4.00

Total $36.00

Transplants Grown

3 each of 10 varieties of tomato 30
2 each of 4 varieties of peppers 8
3 each of 2 varieties of eggplant 6
6 each of 3 varieties of cabbage 18
6 each of 2 varieties of cauliflower 12
6 each of 3 varieties of broccoli 18
6 each of 4 varieties of head lettuce 24
6 each of 2 varieties of celery 12

Total 128

Purchased separately, these same transplants might cost $35 or more. Of course, if your garden is smaller, starting fewer plants would cost proportionally less.

How to Grow Transplants

The following steps for growing your own transplants will work with almost any plant, although some aspects, such as the starting time, will have to be adjusted to suit the vegetable and the last frost date in your area. Also, with some plants, I modify the seed planting technique slightly — for example, tomato plants will root along a buried stem (see Growing Essentials for tomatoes). Thus before using the following instructions, read the section in the book dealing with the vegetable for which you wish to grow transplants.

¶ Organize the seeds. Refer to your garden map and decide how many transplants of each variety you will plant, planning to place similar vegetables close together in the trays (for example, eggplants and peppers). In a small notebook, record the date, the varieties planted, and the source and age of each seed. Be adventuresome and grow a few new varieties each year.

¶ Prepare the planting trays. Obtain planting trays and inserts with 32 to 36 cells in each (cell size: 2 by $2^1/_4$ by $2^1/_4$ inches). I recommend purchasing trays and inserts at a local greenhouse. They buy them in bulk for starting their own seedlings, and you should be able to get a tray and insert for less than 2 dollars. Mail-order companies commonly charge 5 to 6 dollars or more for the same items. I prefer to use plastic trays and inserts because compressed peat or fiber pots dry out too quickly. Wash the trays with soapy water and rinse in a weak solution of bleach and water to kill bacteria or fungal spores that might be present.

(Remember to also clean the tools you use later for transplanting.) Fill each cell to the top with a high-quality starting mix that includes fertilizer (for example, Jiffy-Mix Plus or Burpee Seed-Starting Formula) or a high-quality potting soil (for example, Peters). Do not use cheap all-purpose potting soils or ordinary garden soil. Remember that a good start for your seedlings is critical. Some starting mixes and potting soils include a fungicide to prevent damping-off of seedlings, so be careful not to breathe starting-mix dust. Moisten the mix in the tray by sprinkling it with warm water (I use the kitchen-sink sprayer); repeat this procedure several times to be sure the mix is thoroughly moist. Allow the mix to drain for 5 to 10 minutes.

¶ Label the cells. Using a waterproof felt-tip pen, mark each cell in the trays with the varieties that will be planted. We abbreviate the names by using the first two or three letters of each variety (for example, EGT = Early Girl tomatoes). We also always arrange the plants of each vegetable in alphabetical order in the trays , just in case some of the felt marker washes off. Draw small maps of the trays and record the cell in which each variety was planted. Alternatively, you may want to use small stakes to label each cell, but if you have young children, don't be

surprised if they pull the stakes out at least once.

¶ Plant the seeds. Using the eraser end of a pencil, make a small hole in the moist mix in the middle of each cell. The holes do not need to be very deep — ¹/₄ inch is fine. Place 2 or 3 seeds in each hole (children really enjoy this step!). After checking each hole to be sure it contains seeds, push some moist mix over it. Cover the top of the tray with plastic wrap to keep the seeds moist.

¶ Germinate the transplants under lights. Place the covered trays about 8 inches under lit fluorescent lights. If the seeds germinate in the dark, they will immediately stretch for light when they get above the ground and quickly become "leggy." Use one "warm" (for the red light waves that plants need) and one "cool-white" (for the blue light waves) tube in each fixture. Research has shown that not only can you grow excellent transplants under these lights, but also they are economical to operate and less expensive than the special grow lamps sold in stores. Regular incandescent bulbs will not work, because they do not supply the right quality of light (that is, red and blue wave lengths) needed to grow strong transplants. Of course, if you have a sunlit area, you can grow your plants there, but you may have more difficulty controlling the growing temperature since sunlight will have significant amounts of heat-producing infrared rays.

¶ Grow the transplants in a cool area. Transplants should be grown in a relatively cool area, about 65° to 75°F. Seedlings, especially those of cool-season plants, will be stockier if grown at cooler temperatures. We grow our transplants in the basement.

¶ Adjust the lighting. After the seedlings break through the surface, remove the plastic wrap. Place the lamps about 1 to 2 inches from the top of the plants. Set up a schedule so the lights remain lit at least 14 to 16 hours each day. I turn them on when I get up (7 A.M.) and turn them off after the evening news (10 P.M.), for a total of 15 hours. This schedule is convenient for both me and the plants! If you occasionally forget to turn them off , don't worry; the extra light won't harm the plants. If you wish, you can purchase a special timer to turn the lights on and off, but they are relatively expensive.

¶ Strengthen the seedlings. Set up a small fan to blow across the plants for at least 1 hour every other day. Plants that are moved (or even rubbed) while in the seedling and early stages of growth will develop additional support tissue and therefore be stockier at transplant time.

¶ Fertilize the soil. After 3 weeks, fertilize once a week with a fertilizer you can dissolve in water (for example, Miracle-Gro) with a 15–30–15 formula. Repeat every 8 to 12 days.

¶ Repot the plants if desired. Tomato, pepper, eggplant, and celery plants benefit from being repotted into larger containers at least once during early growth. Do this when they have 3 to 4 true leaves (those developed after the first 2 seed leaves), usually when the plants are 3 to 7 weeks old. Repot them into containers at least twice the size of the originals. Waxed-paper quart or half-gallon milk or juice containers are ideal, but be sure to put a drainage hole in the bottom of each.

¶ Harden the plants. One to two weeks before transplanting them to the garden, begin hardening your transplants. This can be done by placing the plants outside in a small hotbox or other area protected from the wind. For the first day, place them so that they will receive only about 1 to 2 hours of direct sunlight; each day, this can be increased until they can be left in the sun all day. You can leave them outside unless the nighttime low is going to fall below 45°F, in which case, bring them inside. Plants dry out more rapidly outside, so if you leave for a day arrange to have somebody water them if necessary. Also watch for insects on your plants during this period. After your plants have been hardened they are ready to go into the garden. If you transplant small plants (2 to 4 inches tall) into Wallo'Waters you may find that hardening your transplants will not be necessary because conditions inside a Wallo'Water remain mild.

A young tomato plant is transplanted without disturbing its rootball. In the background other transplants are thriving in the protected environment of Wallo'Waters.

15

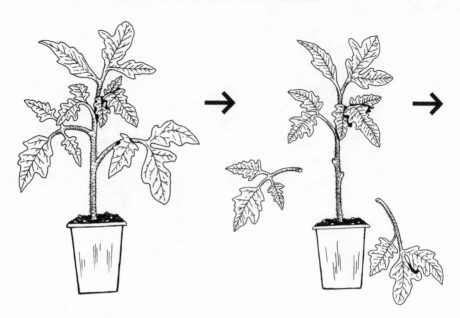

Into the Real World: Transplanting Your Plants

I am convinced that one of the most important factors in assuring maximum production from a plant is the treatment it receives at transplanting. Until this point, each plant has lived in the relative security and comfort of the potting flat. Now seedlings are thrust into the real world of the garden, with its weather, its insects, and so on. If you add to this a poor start, you've got a perfect recipe for failure. Handled with special care at transplanting, your transplants should grow vigorously and provide you with a bountiful harvest. Here's how I generally handle transplanting, but be sure to consult the information under each vegetable for any specific instructions before planting.

¶ Pre-dig each hole and place at least 1 tablespoon of a granular fertilizer (for example, 5–10–5) in the bottom. Firmly cover the fertilizer with at least 2 inches of soil. This extra reserve of fertilizer will be available later as the plant grows.

¶ Place the transplant into a hole and fill it carefully, so as not to disturb the granular fertilizer, with a water-soluble fertilizer mix (for example, 15–30–15). This will provide the roots with an immediate source of nutrients as the plant resumes growth. After the liquid has soaked completely into the rootball and the surrounding soil, pack the earth firmly around each plant.

¶ Feed the transplant with an additional quart or so of water-soluble fertilizer mix.

¶ For protection from the elements, transplant the seedlings into a Wallo'Water or cover plants with hotkaps (waxed-paper cones that fit over the plants). When using Wallo'Waters, you must have them in

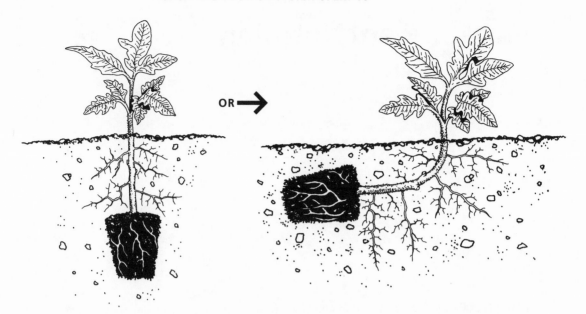

Tomato plants will root along any buried stem, so when transplanting, remove the lower leaves and bury a portion of the stem vertically or horizontally for a stronger plant.

place at least 1 week before transplanting so the soil will be warm. Also, if you place Wallo'Waters on black plastic mulch, be sure the holes you cut in the plastic are large enough to set the Wallo'Waters over bare ground; otherwise the plastic may serve as an insulator and prevent the soil from warming. With hotkaps, anchor the edges with dirt to prevent them from blowing away in strong winds. Wallo'Waters are the most effective protection against frost and, in fact, will even protect the transplants from a hard freeze or unexpected spring snows. I've had radishes in one that survived outside overnight lows of 8°F! These remarkable devices can also be used for extra-early starts (2 months) since they capture and release both solar energy and latent energy of fusion of water (as much as 900,000 calories of heat in a single Wallo'Water as the water freezes), thus creating a favorable environment for plant growth in the interior of the Wallo'Water. I do not recommend coffee cans or the like because they are not light transparent, and I discourage the use of plastic milk jugs because they are difficult to keep anchored in a windy region. Hotkaps are inexpensive (about 10 to 30 cents each) and are biodegradable and can be tilled into the soil. Although Wallo'Waters are more expensive (about $3 each), they provide more protection and, with reasonable care, can be reused for several years. Start seedlings extra early if you intend to use Wallo'Waters.
¶ Pay attention to the last spring and first fall frost dates (see the photographs on pages 55–56) when transplanting. Information concerning the application of these dates is given in this book under each vegetable.

Chapter Three

Plant Nutrition

Using Fertilizers When you consider that most vegetables go through their entire life cycle from germination to fruit production in as little as a few months, you can appreciate the importance of understanding the mineral requirements of plants. Knowing the functions of minerals can help you grow healthy plants, and lets you get the best production from any particular vegetable. Thirteen minerals, sometimes referred to as the macro- and micronutrients, are essential to good plant growth. Of the macronutrients, nitrogen (N), phosphorus (P), and potassium (K) are the ones most rapidly depleted from soils. For this reason, formulas on fertilizer containers list percentages of N-P-K, in that order (for example, 15–30–15 or 27–3–3). These formulas are important to the gardener for another reason: They allow him or her to directly compare fertilizers. For example, 10 pounds of a 5–10–5 fertilizer are essentially equal to 5 pounds of a 10–20–10 fertilizer. Since other minerals may be deficient in some soils, it is not unusual to find fertilizers supplemented with such minerals as iron (Fe) or copper (Cu).

Consider especially the roles of nitrogen, phosphorus, and potassium when growing vegetables. Nitrogen is needed by the plant to manufacture many of the materials it uses to form stems and leaves. Because nitrogen is a highly mobile mineral, it is rapidly lost from the soil through leaching and the bacterial decomposition of organic matter, and generally must be replenished more frequently than other minerals. Too little nitrogen and the plant is stunted and matures poorly; too much and you'll see lush growth of stems and leaves but few flowers and fruits.

Phosphorus is found in the membrane surrounding every plant cell and plays a key role in the manufacture of sugars during photosynthesis. Compared with nitrogen and potassium, phosphorus doesn't move much through the soil and, as a rule, must be placed close to the plant roots. Seedlings, especially, benefit from phosphorus, and using phosphorus-rich liquid starter solutions at transplanting time insures a better start. Plants lacking phosphorus are often stunted, exhibit a purplish tinge, and produce fewer flowers and fruits. Since excess phosphorus is rapidly tied up in the soil in unavailable forms, an overabundance of this mineral is rarely a problem.

Potassium, the last of the big three, assists the plant in root growth and in the opening and closing of breathing pores (stomata) on leaves. A deficiency results in plants with weak root systems, poorly developed stems and leaves, and reduced yields. An overabundance of potassium is generally not harmful to plants, although potassium salts should not be placed next to newly planted seeds or transplant roots. Occasionally, too much potassium can interfere with the uptake of magnesium, an important element in chlorophyll, the pigment needed in photosynthesis.

How can this information about minerals be used in growing vegetables? When applying granular fertilizers at planting or side-dressing time, ask yourself what parts of the plant you will be harvesting to eat and the roles of particular minerals in the development of those parts. The Fertilizer Guide lists the parts of each plant that are eaten and examples of fertilizers I have found useful in maximizing production.

Fertilizer Guide for Vegetables

Vegetable	Part Eaten	Fertilizer
Asparagus	Stems	8–10–8, 0–20–0
Beans	Fruits and Seeds	5–10–5, 8–10–8, 4–12–12
Beets	Roots and Leaves	5–10–5, 8–10–8, 4–12–12
Broccoli	Flowers	8–10–8, 8–22–6, 4–12–12
Cabbage	Leaves and Seeds	27–3–3, 8–10–8
Carrots	Roots	8–10–8, 0–20–0, 4–12–12
Cauliflower	Flowers	8–10–8, 8–22–6
Celery	Stems and Leaves	27–3–3, 8–10–8
Corn	Seeds	8–10–8, 8–22–6
Cucumber	Fruits	8–10–8, 8–22–6
Eggplant	Fruits	8–10–8, 8–22–6
Lettuce	Leaves	27–3–3, 8–10–8
Muskmelon	Fruits	8–10–8, 8–22–6
Okra	Fruits	8–10–8, 8–22–6

Onions	Leaves	8–10–8, 8–22–6
Peanuts	Seeds	5–10–5, 8–10–8, 4–12–12
Peas	Fruits and Seeds	8–10–8, 8–22–6
Peppers	Fruits	8–10–8, 8–22–6
Potatoes	Stems	8–10–8, 8–22–6
Pumpkins	Fruits	8–10–8, 8–22–6
Radishes	Roots	8–10–8, 0–20–0
Rhubarb	Leaf Stalks	8–10–8, 0–20–0
Spinach	Leaves	27–3–3, 8–10–8
Squash	Fruits	8–10–0, 8–22–6
Strawberries	Fruits	8–10–8, 8–22–6
Sweet potatoes	Roots	8–10–8, 0–20–0
Tomatoes	Fruits	8–10–8, 8–22–6
Watermelons	Fruits	8–10–8, 8–22–6

As you can see, with cabbage or lettuce you will be harvesting mostly leaves, so a high-nitrogen fertilizer (for example, 27–3–3) encourages abundant leaf growth. With tomatoes or broccoli you will be eating fruits or flower clusters, so a high-phosphorus fertilizer (for example, 8–22–6) would be helpful. Usually, I apply 2 to 4 pounds of the appropriate fertilizer in each 10-by-10-foot area and mix it with the upper 6 to 8 inches of soil prior to planting. However, don't add fertilizers if a soil test indicates that they are not necessary. Keep in mind that you can always side-dress later and that anytime during the season, a vegetable will benefit from a soaking with a water-soluble fertilizer.

In addition to chemical fertilizers, organic materials, such as leaves, manure, or compost, may be used in order to add nutrients to the soil, although these materials generally have a weaker analysis (for example, 1–2–1) than chemical fertilizers. The decomposition of organics may also significantly deplete minerals like nitrogen from the soil. The use of cover crops such as peas and beans, which actually add nitrogen to the soil, can help to control the problem of nitrogen loss. Consult additional sources (for example, The National Garden Association's *Gardening*) for the use of compost and cover crops.

Soil pH   Technically, pH is a measure of the number of hydrogen ions (H+) present in the soil. Soils with a high number of these hydrogen ions are acidic (pH of 2 [highly acidic] to 6.9 [very slightly acidic]), and soils with low numbers of hydrogen ions are alkaline (pH of 7.1 [very slightly alkaline] to 12 [highly alkaline]). Soils in dry regions tend to be alkaline, whereas soils in wet climates tend to be acidic. Other factors that influence pH include rainfall (most is acidic and lowers pH), fertilizers (tend to make soils acidic), high levels of organic matter (pine needles in the Colorado foothills, for instance, tend to promote acidic soils), and the types of rocks from which a soil is formed (limestone rocks in much of Kansas and other areas in the Heartland, for instance, promote alkaline soils). Thus, when I gardened in Kansas, my soil pH was initially 8.5, but in Colorado it was 5.5. I eventually added nearly 40 pounds of iron sulfate ($FeSO_4$) to lower the soil pH in my 20-by-55-foot Kansas garden, and lime ($CaCO_3$) to raise the soil pH in my Colorado garden. It is important to understand that soil pH generally does not change suddenly or drastically under normal conditions.

Plants do not grow well in either highly acidic or highly alkaline soils; rather, they generally do best when the pH is between 5.5 and 7.5 (7 is neutral). A few exhibit better growth in acidic soils (for example, 4.5–5.5 for potatoes, watermelon, and rhubarb), while others grow better in less acidic and alkaline soils (for example, 6.5–7.5 for cole crops, beets, lettuce, onions, and asparagus).

Of considerable importance to gardening and plant nutrition is that the availability of mineral nutrients to plants is governed by soil pH. Nitrogen, phosphorus, and potassium are readily available under neutral, slightly acidic, or slightly alkaline conditions (pH 6.5–7.5), but become less so as the pH becomes more acidic. Other minerals (for example, calcium and magnesium) are more available under alkaline conditions (pH 7.0–8.5); still others (for example, iron, copper, manganese, boron, and zinc) are more available under acidic conditions (pH 4.5–6.5).

If you are like most gardeners, you have probably never tested your soil pH. However, knowing what it is, and what needs to be done to modify it, can help you increase the general health and productivity of the plants in your garden. I would advise you, therefore, to have the pH checked every 4 to 5 years. You can do this by submitting soil samples to local or state extension folks, or check the pH yourself by using testing kits that are usually available in garden centers.

Chapter Four **Mulches**

Using mulches in the garden is nothing new. As long ago as the seventeenth century, books mentioned covering the garden with straw and cloth to maintain the health of the plants and the soil. Although some of the materials used for mulches have changed dramatically over the centuries, the reasons for using mulch have hardly changed at all. We use it in the garden primarily to conserve soil moisture, to control soil temperatures, and to prevent weed growth. Mulch application must be considered carefully, however, in order not to cancel beneficial advantages in one area with disadvantages in another. The following information and tips should help you to use mulches in a manner that will maximize their benefits.

¶ Different mulches affect soil temperature differently. All mulches conserve soil moisture, but they differ considerably in their effect on soil temperature. I like to think of mulches as being divided into two types, cooling and heating, depending on whether they lower or raise the soil temperature. Cooling mulches, such as straw, grass, leaf clippings, paper, and, less commonly, aluminum foil, lower the temperature of the soil as much as 10°F by preventing sunlight from striking the surface. Heating mulches, such as plastic films, allow the sunlight to strike the soil directly, thereby heating it by as much as 10°F.

¶ Tailor the type and timing of mulches to the crop. Cool-season crops like broccoli and potatoes do best in a cool soil, and cooling mulches often can be applied soon after the crops become established in the spring. However, warm-season crops like squash, tomatoes, and eggplants require a warm soil to thrive; applying a warming plastic film when planting these crops in the late spring helps them to get off to a good start. If you choose not to use plastic mulches for warm-weather crops, do not apply a cooling, organic mulch until June 15 or after, to insure that the soil has been warmed thoroughly. Although soil temperatures will drop just after applying a cooling mulch, they will not fall below temperatures for optimum root growth since air temperatures will remain high.

¶ Use plastic mulch to get an early start and yield. Get an early start in the spring by using plastic mulches to warm the soil. Have them in place at least 7 to 10 days prior to planting. You can then plant seeds or transplants through holes cut in the plastic. Later, if the soil gets too warm under the plastic, you can cover it with a layer of straw or grass. A Kansas State University (KSU) study in southeastern Kansas showed that using plastic mulches with muskmelons resulted in earlier harvests but not necessarily total yields for a season. In the same study, the use of a floating row cover with a clear-plastic mulch resulted in even earlier yields. KSU researchers, in a 2-year study in northwestern Kansas, found that using plastic mulches with tomatoes produced significantly heavier total season yields. Mulches of clear plastic proved superior.

¶ Take your soil's temperature. Most seeds germinate best between 75° and 85°F, and most plants grow best when the soil temperature is around 70°F. If you are using a warming plastic mulch, you can either use a soil thermometer to know exactly when to plant your seeds or cover the plastic later with a cooling, organic mulch so the soil doesn't get too warm. Because some cool-season vegetables, such as lettuce, can be planted in the early spring when the soil temperature reaches about

55°F, a soil thermometer can alert you to the proper time to plant.

¶ Select mulches carefully for pest control. If you have trouble with white grubs, cutworms, crickets, and pill bugs, which usually eat ripe fruit, plastic mulches can provide a barrier between the plant and the soil that significantly reduces problems with these pests. On the other hand, thick layers of organic mulch, such as straw, will usually increase the number of these pests in your garden. If you use organic mulches, keep fruits supported so they don't rest on the mulch.

¶ Use mulches for weed control. Plastic mulches effectively prevent weed growth by creating conditions (for example, excess heat and/or reduced light) that usually kill the weeds. Don't worry that weeds seem at first to thrive under the plastic — too much of a good thing will eventually do them in. Organic mulches that are applied after weeds have been controlled by other methods (see chapter 6) will prevent further growth by shutting off their access to sunlight.

¶ Use mulches to slow water loss. Mulches effectively slow evaporation of water from the soil surface and thus play a critical role in water conservation in the garden.

¶ Consider the cost and disposal of mulches. When deciding on a mulch, remember that organic mulches (straw, grass clippings, and so on) are generally free or inexpensive and can be tilled into the soil in the fall. Plastic films and woven materials are more costly and cannot be tilled into the soil. Plastic films can also be a real mess if they disintegrate late in the season, as happened to me one year in South Dakota. Some woven materials can be used for several seasons.

Bean leaf beetle

Chapter Five Pest and Disease Control

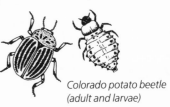
Colorado potato beetle (adult and larvae)

Consider Your Options

Asparagus beetle

It would be nice to think that your garden will be the one that is missed by pests and disease. Forget it! At some point in your gardening career, you will want to control an infestation of a particular pest or disease. You must then make some important decisions. For example, if you choose to use pesticides (any product used to destroy, prevent, or control pests), then you'll need to decide whether to use only natural types or a combination of natural and synthetic types. The best advice I can offer is to first educate yourself to the alternatives.

If you decide not to use sprays or powders for pest and disease control, you have several options, which I call collectively the biological-mechanical, or biomech, approach. First, you can simply pick the grasshoppers, squash bugs, and so on, off the plants and either crush them or drown them in a jar of rubbing alcohol. However, this method may not be suitable for the squeamish, and anyone who has chased large, yellow, tomato-eating grasshoppers knows how difficult catching them can be. Use caution when picking insects to avoid grabbing potentially harmful ones, such as blister beetles and certain wasps. Second, you may use a program of companion planting, that is, putting plants together in the garden that are reputed to repel insects from each other (for example, marigolds among your beans). Although controlling pests in this manner would ultimately be ideal, it is time-consuming and, in many cases, of questionable value. My success with it has been very limited and often spectacularly counterproductive. For example, I once attracted huge numbers of aphids with radishes that I had companion planted with spinach to repel chewing pests; another time, I created a natural haven for grasshoppers by companion planting asparagus and tomatoes, causing severe damage to both vegetables! The moral? Don't be afraid to try companion planting but do so with care (see *Carrots Love Tomatoes*, in Annotated Bibliography).

Third, you can purchase and introduce beneficial insects (for example, praying mantises, ladybugs, and green lacewings) and bacteria

Cabbage looper

Cutworm

Grasshopper

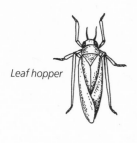

Leaf hopper

into your garden and, in some cases, encourage their continued presence. Praying mantises, for example, are relatively easy to establish in a garden, and by driving 1-by-1-inch untreated, weathered, wooden stakes into the ground among your garden plants in the late summer and fall, you will encourage mantises to lay egg masses on the stakes. The stakes and attached egg cases can then be stored in an unheated garage or shed during the winter and returned to the garden in the late spring. When they hatch, you'll have literally hundreds of mantises guarding your vegetables, eating moths, grasshoppers, crickets, and many other pests.

Finally, you can purchase traps that attract and trap offending insects or use barriers, such as fleece, that physically keep insects away. Be careful when using these traps, because they contain powerful substances that may attract pests that might otherwise not be there. Don't use a trap if there is no evidence that a particular pest is around! I use the biomech approach whenever possible. I would caution you that plants with diseases such as wilts cannot be saved, and keeping them around will only spread the disease. Diseased plants should be destroyed immediately.

The second approach you have to pest and disease

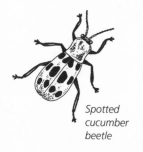

Spotted cucumber beetle

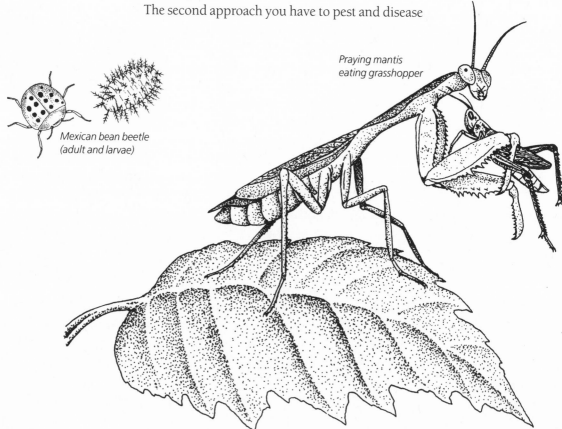

Mexican bean beetle (adult and larvae)

Praying mantis eating grasshopper

Squash vine borer

control is to use a naturally based pesticide. "Natural" does not mean "non-poisonous"; rather, the product either is composed of bacterial spores or is made from naturally occurring minerals or extracts from plants. Some, such as pyrethrum, have been used for more than three hundred years. In addition to their ability to kill or control insects and diseases, these products break down readily in the environment and do not accumulate in the soil. Unlike many synthetic products, natural pesticides do not build up in the body cells of warm-blooded animals, including man. All can be used up to the day of harvest, but you should wash any treated vegetables thoroughly before eating. Better safe than sorry! In the past, these natural controls have sometimes been difficult to purchase at many stores, but attention has recently focused on the side effects of many synthetic chemicals in our environment, making the use of natural products more attractive; they are generally more available now (for sources, see the National Gardening Association's *Directory of Seed and Nursery Catalogs* in the Annotated Bibliography). If your local garden center does not carry them, let them know that you want them — educate them.

Flea beetle

The third approach to pest and disease control is to use synthetic products. Still the main choice of control by many gardeners, these powerful poisons are attractive because generally they kill and control pests and diseases longer than the other methods. Unfortunately, many of these poisons have not been around for very long and their exact effects on other living organisms, including humans, are unknown. Some that were once sold widely and recommended for use in home gardens have since been shown to cause serious health problems in humans and other animals and consequently have been removed from the market. As I indicated previously, one such product, chlordane, was commonly sold for insect control on vegetables and weed control on lawns! Another widely recommended and used synthetic insecticide, kelthane, is currently under review by the Environmental Protection Agency.

Weevil

The last approach for controlling pests and diseases combines the methods of the first three. This approach has been referred to as integrated pest management (IPM). Remember that whatever approach you use, you should rotate your crops every year to protect against any diseases or pests that might overwinter in the soil.

Squash bug

Know Your Enemies and Your Friends

A famous general once remarked that most battles are won by the commander who knows the most about his enemy. This is good advice for the garden as well. Be sure you know what disease or pest is attack-

27

ing your plants. Some common pests are shown on pp. 25–27. Before taking any action, you should learn about beneficial insects. Obtain a good book or magazine that identifies both beneficial and harmful insects (see Annotated Bibliography) and take the time to learn to recognize both.

Many such books provide colored pictures of the pests and diseases, as well as information for their natural or synthetic control. There is also considerable information available on these subjects at your local library and agricultural extension office. Most states publish pamphlets or books on vegetable pests and diseases and their control that are available to the public free (most) or at low cost. Unfortunately, many of these publications emphasize synthetic products for control. If you decide not to use sprays or powders, or choose to use only natural products, you may have to purchase specialized books on subjects such as organic gardening.

I have provided a key (p. 36) and guide (p. 40) to help you identify common pest and disease problems of garden plants. If after using this key and guide and consulting other books, you still can't identify a plant pest or disease, collect a sample and take it to your extension agent for identification. He or she will either identify it or send it to a university for identification; usually you will not be charged for this service. Be sure to provide the agent with a fresh specimen; if necessary, preserve it in a vial of rubbing alcohol (don't, however, send the vial through the mail).

Beneficial Insects in the Garden

Many beneficial insects inhabit most gardens. These insects destroy a large number of pests, and if you use insecticides, you may kill both the good and the bad insects. Therefore, it is essential that you know what insect you have seen before using any insecticide. It might be one of the good gals or guys! The following beneficial insects can be found in most gardens.

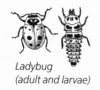

*Ladybug
(adult and larvae)*

Ladybugs. These beautiful little insects come in several varieties. Although the one familiar to most gardeners is the orange or red form with black spots, there are spotless orange, gray to pale yellow, and even black forms. The immature stage is a small ($1/4$ to $1/2$ inch long), wrinkled, spindle-shaped larva that is black with orange spots. Ladybugs are especially fond of aphids but will also eat mites and other soft-bodied insects and the eggs and larvae of many insects.

Lacewings. These graceful insects are slender, green or brownish creatures with transparent wings; they are about a $1/2$ inch long. The larval form in one variety is the ant lion, which makes conical depressions in fine sand and silt (great to show young gardeners). The form found most often in vegetable gardens is the green lacewing, which lays its tiny white eggs on slender stalks on stems or on the bottom sides of leaves. Lacewings feed on aphids and the eggs of other insects.

Bees. Whether a honey bee or a bumble bee, these industrious insects are extremely important in causing pollination in many vegetables. Unlike wasps, bees are generally fuzzy and do not eat other insects.

Wasps. Two types of beneficial wasps are generally seen in the garden: the social wasps, such as the familiar yellow jackets, and the nonsocial ones, such as the braconids, chalcids, ichneumons, and trichogrammas. Yellow jackets often feed on small insects and worms such as cabbage loopers, thereby playing a valuable role in ridding the garden of pests. The less familiar nonsocial types are small, colorful flying insects that deposit their eggs on various pests. The eggs hatch, and the wasp larvae feed on and eventually kill the insect. The pests that these wasps attack include aphids, various worms and caterpillars, whiteflies, leafhoppers, and some beetles. Little wonder that these wasps are extremely valuable pest control insects.

Spiders. Technically, spiders are not insects, but they are certainly beneficial creatures in the garden. I have been especially impressed watching wolf and crab spiders as they captured and ate white cabbage butterflies, eliminating many future generations of worms that might eat holes in my cole crops.

Praying Mantises. The praying mantis (or mantid) is so named because of its habit of folding its legs prayerlike in front of its body. It is a very efficient predatory insect that will capture and consume any garden insect, beneficial and nonbeneficial alike. However, in my experience, I have seen them eat more pests than nonpests, and I consider them an important garden friend. Showing and explaining mantises to children is a wonderful way to give youngsters an appreciation for the intricacies of nature and a way to calm fears they might have about insects.

Other, less common, beneficial garden insects include fireflies; ground beetles; pirate bugs; robber flies; rove, soldier, and tiger beetles; and hover and trachinid flies.

All of the beneficial insects I have described should encourage us to be less prone to immediately spray the garden with a chemical when we see or suspect a pest. Many helpful insects can now be purchased from greenhouses or through seed and nursery catalogs for release in gardens.

Pesticide Safety   Whether you use a natural (organic, if plant derived; inorganic, if derived from sources such as rocks) or synthetic (man-made) pesticide,

Did You Know?
Insect Structures and Patterns

The Beautiful
One of the most enjoyable aspects of being both a gardener and a professionally trained scientist is that I frequently get to enjoy the structural complexity and beauty of all types of biological organisms. Insects, both beneficial and harmful, are especially good subjects to study at the microscopic level. Although we may strive to save the mantis as we destroy the squash bug, we can enjoy the beauty found on both.

The Practical
Many insects, such as praying mantises, are extremely important to the health of the garden, which suggests that the gardener should be extremely careful when using any insecticide. Read labels and consider fully the effects of nonselective insecticides on the complex, unseen world in the garden. Understanding the world around and below us is the best defense against pests and disease.

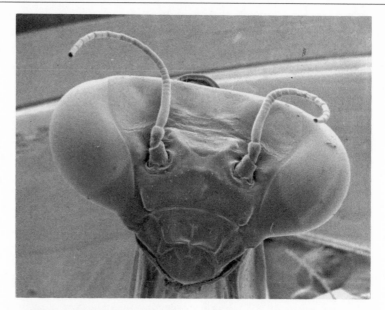

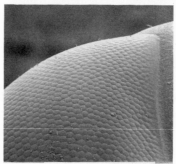

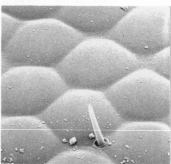

One of the most remarkable creatures in the garden is the praying mantis (head at top, magnified 15 times), a very efficient, and usually beneficial, predatory insect. Its victims include almost any insect that comes within its reach, particularly such destructive ones as grasshoppers, moths, and crickets. The tremendous number of facets (six-sided sections) in a mantis's eyes (lower left, magnified 110 times) allows it to see much better than many other insects in the garden. Further, special sensory hairs in the mantis's eyes (lower right, magnified 1,000 times) enable it to literally feel with its eyes! The mantis is the tiger of the garden.

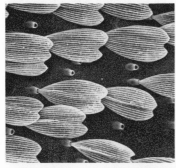

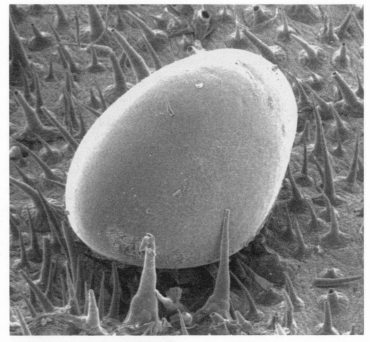

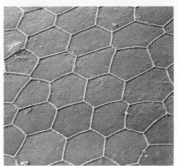

Even the disgusting squash bug possesses a beauty of its own. A squash bug egg is attached to a mass of pointed hairs on a squash leaf (top right, magnified 48 times). Upon closer inspection (bottom right, magnified 350 times) one can see an intriguing geometric pattern on the egg's surface that helps to strengthen it.

Although the wings of moths and butterflies appear smooth, they are actually covered with small, intricate scales. Close examination of the wing surface of an orange-collared moth (top left, magnified 26 times) shows a silvery layer that when further enlarged (middle left, magnified 320 times, and bottom left, magnified 3,000 times) reveals individual scales attached to the wing much like the feathers of a bird. If you have ever captured a butterfly or moth, only to have them struggle and escape, you know they often leave a slippery, grayish powder on your hands. This material is actually thousands of scales released readily from the wing, providing the butterfly or moth with an effective escape mechanism!

it is extremely important to use them safely.

¶ At the risk of sounding like a broken record: Read labels carefully! The label will give you vital information about mixing the product (if necessary), what pest, disease, or weed the product will control, possible health effects, and so on. One of the most serious instances of pesticide misuse that I have witnessed was when a friend became quite ill because he improperly used Orthene on his tomato plants. He had not read the label fully, because it clearly indicates that Orthene should not be used on vegetables.

¶ When mixing and applying, wear proper clothing — for example, a long-sleeved shirt, plastic gloves (cheap dish-washing types are fine), and a breathing mask (an inexpensive dust cloth or light towel wrapped around the face will do). While powdered products such as sabadilla and rotenone have low acute toxicity to mammals, breathing them may produce serious side effects. Mix all products in a well-ventilated area, and do not allow unprotected individuals, especially children, to be nearby during mixing or application. Be sure not to get bacterial biological controls in open cuts.

¶ Apply only under appropriate weather conditions. It is only common sense not to apply a product when the wind is blowing 20 miles per hour, yet I have seen this happen more than once. The best time to apply these products is generally toward the evening when winds are usually calm (your rotenone dust will not blow away), when beneficial insects such as bees are out of the garden (critical if a product like Sevin is used), and when hot sunlight will not be a major factor (sunlight kills the beneficial bacteria, for example, *Bt*). Some pesticides (for example, sulfur) will damage plants if they are applied when temperatures are too high.

¶ Wash everything thoroughly after each use. Clean yourself and your mixing and application tools and wash any clothing that has been worn during application.

¶ Store the products safely out of the reach of children. I put mine in a secure boxed area where they cannot be easily reached, and where they cannot be accidentally knocked off a shelf. Also, be sure that this place is away from living areas, preferably in a detached garage or shed. I always cringe when I walk into stores and smell the heavy aroma of pesticides in their garden sections, because I know that the store employees are breathing these products every day.

¶ Dispose of unwanted products and empty containers properly. Completely empty containers can be wrapped in newspaper and placed in the trash. Do not wash any of these products, natural or synthetic, down the drain, because many are deadly to fish. Check with your local extension agent to determine the proper way to dispose of unused pesticides in your community.

Products I Use in My Vegetable Garden

For many years, I used a wide assortment of natural and synthetic pesticides to eliminate or control pests and diseases in my gardens. However, over the years as I became more aware of the complexity and interaction of living organisms in my gardens, I began to look for ways to reduce my dependence on synthetic chemicals to treat pests and diseases. Although I don't feel that I'll ever be able to garden entirely without the use of any pesticides (pests and diseases are persistent), I am convinced that being selective and knowing about the products I do use best protects my family and the beneficial organisms in my garden against possible side effects. I now use only the following nonsynthetic pesticides to treat pests and diseases in my gardens.

Rotenone. Derived from a South American plant, rotenone is highly effective against a number of chewing insects, which eat the powder, sicken, and die. I use this to kill many pests, including flea beetles (radishes, cole crops, and eggplants), cucumber beetles (vine crops, beans, and eggplants), squash vine borers (squash), Colorado potato beetle, especially larvae (potatoes), Mexican bean beetle (beans), and pill bugs or roly-polies (various crops). Most beneficial insects, such as praying mantises, are not affected by rotenone. It is available usually in 1 percent and 5 percent formulations for dusting; I generally use the 1 percent mix.

Pyrethrum. This insecticide, made from the flowers of a type of daisy, is highly effective against a broad spectrum of insects (the synthetic duplicate is called pyrethrin). I use it especially for thrips (broccoli and other vegetables), squash bugs and squash vine borers and their eggs (vine crops), grasshoppers (all crops), weevils (carrots, turnips, and cabbage), and asparagus beetles. A significant disadvantage of this product is that it will also kill beneficial insects such as mantises and ladybugs.

Insecticidal soaps. Composed of fatty acid compounds that are often associated with detergents, these products are special formulations that have been approved for use in gardens. Although they are sometimes compared to dishwashing detergents, this is inaccurate because house-hold detergents frequently contain many other substances (such as fragrances and coloring agents) besides fatty acid compounds. I have used insecticidal soaps quite effectively to control aphids, whiteflies, and mites on beans, eggplants, tomatoes, and other vegetables.

Sabadilla. Derived from the seeds of a South American plant, this powder is very effective in controlling squash bugs, especially in the adult stage. It also controls cucumber beetles, leafhoppers, and cabbage loopers. Sabadilla is relatively expensive but a must if other controls fail.

Bordeaux mixture. This product consists of copper sulfate and lime, and has been used since the mid-1800s for controlling fungal diseases. It is very poisonous if it is inhaled or swallowed, and the label instructions should be followed carefully. I use it because, when it is mixed with water and used as a spray, it is highly effective in controlling fungal (leaf spots, blights, downy and powdery mildews, and anthracnose) and some bacterial diseases (bacterial spots) on tomatoes, potatoes, and vine crops.

Sulfur. One of the basic elements, sulfur can be applied in the garden as dust or spray (my preference) on tomatoes to control mites. It should not be used, however, if the tomatoes will be canned in metal contain-ers. Sulfur is also effective in controlling powdery mildews on beans, peas, and squash.

Bacillus thuringiensis (Bt). This is actually a species of bacteria (several varieties are now known) that is eaten by the pest; as such, *Bt* is considered a biological pest control. After ingesting the bacterium, most pests sicken, stop feeding within 30 minutes, and die within 24 hours. *Bt* is sold as a powder (BT or Dipel) or liquid (Thuricide) to control a wide variety of worms, caterpillars, and borers, and as a liquid (M-1 and Trident) to control Colorado potato beetle. I use it to control especially looper and cabbage worms (broccoli, cauliflower, and cabbage), tomato fruitworms, and corn earworms. It will also kill large tomato hornworms if they become a problem.

Bacillus popilliae (Bp). This is a bacterium that causes milky spore disease in the white grubs that are the "worm" stages of June beetles and Japanese beetles.

Nosema locustae (Nl). A bacterium that causes grasshoppers to sicken and die. Applied to the garden, it can be effective for several years.

A Special Grass-hopper Cocktail

Over the years, grasshoppers have been a common problem in my Heartland gardens, especially in Kansas, Iowa, and Texas. These pests can rapidly overrun and destroy plants; it takes only a small number of them to cause significant damage to individual vegetables. Nothing is more irritating than picking a large, ripe tomato only to find that one or more of those large yellow grasshoppers has chewed holes in it! I control grasshoppers in my gardens in three ways. First, if they are not too abundant, I catch and destroy them by hand. I do not recommend this method for the squeamish or less agile gardener. Second, I recently applied spores of *Nosema locustae* to one of my gardens in the hope of decreasing the grasshopper population. Although it is too early to know for sure, it does appear that fewer of these pests are around compared with previous years. Finally, when grasshopper populations get out of control, I resort to a "cocktail" of natural pesticides that I prepare and spray on the offenders. Mix together 18 ounces of water, 4 ounces of .02 percent pyrethrum spray (commonly available in garden centers), and 1 tablespoon of insecticidal soap. This solution will kill (by direct contact) even large yellow grasshoppers.

Common Synthetic Pesticides

I do not use or recommend the use of synthetic products in any home garden. However, these pest and disease control products are extremely common on many store shelves, and are likely to be there for some time to come. For this reason, I feel it is important for a gardener to understand some facts about these products.

Table 5.1 Common Synthetic Pesticides

Name	Pest or Disease Controlled	Waiting Period before Eating Vegetables / Comments
Insecticides		
Diazinon	Various insects	7 (beans) to 35 days (potatoes); sometimes used as a soil insecticide
Malathion	Various insects and some mites	1 (beans) to 14 days (lettuce); reported to be one of the least toxic to mammals, including humans
Methoxychlor	Various insects	3 (beans) to 14 days (carrots); overuse may cause buildup of aphids; do not use on cucurbits
Sevin	Various insects	0 (beans) to 14 days (lettuce); very toxic to bees
Fungicides		
Benomyl	Fungi	0 (melons) to 28 days (lima beans); not for use on all vegetables, so read label carefully
Chlorothalonil	Fungi	0 (most vegetables) to 14 (corn); not for use on all vegetables, so read label carefully
Maneb	Fungi	0 (beans) to 14 days (celery)
Zineb	Fungi	0 (corn) to 10 days (lettuce)

Table 5.2 Key to Common Pest, Disease, and Physiological Problems of Vegetable Plants

This key can help identify common vegetable plant problems. To determine the nature of the problem, always begin with the two key steps labeled "1." Say, for example, that your tomatoes have circular, dime-sized sunken areas with small black spots in the center. Since tomatoes are a fruit, you select the first step 1: "Fruits, heads, cobs, bulbs, or roots damaged." The "2" at the end of the line directs you to key steps 2, where you repeat the process, selecting the step that best describes your problem — in this case, the first step 2: "Fruits, cobs, or heads damaged." You continue sequentially through the steps until you end up at the second step 11: "Round, watery sunken spots (often with a dark center) on fruits (Z)." The "Z" refers to description Z (p. 42) in the Gardener's Guide to Vegetable Plant Problems and Suggested Treatments (Table 5.3), where you learn what the problem is (anthracnose) and how to treat it. This key and the Gardener's Guide will enable you to quickly identify common vegetable plant problems and determine appropriate treatment for them.

1. Fruits, heads, cobs, bulbs, or roots damaged 2
1. Leaves, stalks, and/or stems damaged 13
    2. Fruits, cobs, or heads damaged 3
    2. Roots or bulbs damaged 12

36

3. Holes in fruits, cobs, or heads 4

3. Other problems with fruits, cobs, or heads 7

    4. Tomato damage 5

    4. Other plants 6

5. Tomatoes, green (V)

5. Tomatoes, ripe (W)

    6. Beans (F)

    6. Cabbage and lettuce (G, H)

    6. Corn (S)

    6. Peppers and strawberries (T)

7. Cracks on fruits or heads or grayish to black masses on cobs 8

7. Spots on fruits or mottled ripening of fruit 9

    8. Cabbage (cracks) (CC)

    8. Corn (grayish masses) (JJ)

    8. Tomatoes (cracks) (BB)

9. Irregular (often mottled) ripening of fruit (tomatoes and cucumbers) (AA)

9. Spots on green or ripe fruits 10

    10. Spots, small (many $1/4$ inch or less wide), round or irregular
        (U,Y)

    10. Spots, larger (to $1/2$ inch wide), irregular and brown to round
        with dark center 11

11. Brown, leathery-looking spots on peppers (X)

11. Round, watery, sunken spots (often with dark center) on fruits (Z)

11. Irregular leathery to soft area at bottom of tomato or pepper (DD)

    12. Carrots (KK)

    12. Potatoes (LL, NN)

    12. Onions (OO)

    12. Radishes (T)

13. Seedling wilts or dies quickly or grows poorly; older plant dies
    quickly 14

13. Plant grows but shows signs of damage, disease or other problem 16

    14. Seedling dies suddenly 15

    14. Older plant wilts and dies suddenly (HH)

15. Young plant cuts off at base (EE)

15. Young plant constricted at base but not cut off; or young plant does
    not grow much (FF, GG)

    16. Leaves with holes or leaves stripped entirely 17

    16. Leaves with spots, yellowish or brownish, or other damage . 19

17. Leaves stripped (M, N)

17. Leaves and/or stalks with holes 18

18. Beans, cucumber (F)
18. Broccoli, cabbage, cauliflower (C, D)
18. Celery (KK)
18. Corn (S, II)
18. Eggplant, radishes (D, F)
18. Lettuce (H)
18. Potato (O)
18. Rhubarb (E)
19. Edges of leaves darkened or burned (lettuce) (P)
19. Problems of plants other than lettuce 20
    20. Leaves, green but shriveled and sometimes sticky, rolled at the edges, or folded together 21
    20. Leaves, with spots, yellowish or brownish, or with a whitish coating 22
21. Tomatoes (Q,R)
21. Strawberry (K)
21. Other plants (Q)
    22. Leaves, with whitish, powdery spots or small whitish flies (A)
    22. Leaves, yellowish or brownish with brown spots or with whitish, cobwebby coating 23
23. Leaves, yellowish or brownish to whitish 24
23. Leaves, with brown spots 25
    24. Tomato, lower leaves yellow and die, starting at the bottom of the plant; plant eventually dies (L)
    24. Corn, lower part of leaves and nodes yellow and weaken (II)
    24. Potatoes, margins of leaves brown and curled (MM)
    24. Various plants, leaves, yellowish or brownish to whitish, often cobwebby on bottom; tiny canoe-shaped (leafhoppers, thrips) or oval (mites, red spiders) pests present (B)
25. Spots with concentric rings; sometimes large (up to ½ inch wide) (J)
25. Spots without rings, usually small (I)

The Really Big Pests   One category of Heartland pests that are sometimes quite troublesome and especially difficult to deal with are what I call the really big pests: deer, rabbits, raccoons, and birds. Although few gardeners in the Great Plains have probably had to deal with all of these, I would guess that the majority have had problems with at least one pesky member of the group at least once. Here are my suggestions for dealing with the critters that most commonly create trouble in Heartland gardens.

Deer. About the only vegetable deer don't seem to like are cucurbits, probably because of their scratchy nature (see Did You Know? Plant

Hairs, page 68). Even spraying spicy concoctions on the plants doesn't discourage these animals. I have found that, short of tying the dog next to the garden, a physical barrier seems to be the only way to keep deer from decimating exposed portions of a garden. You could erect an electric fence such as those sold by garden supply houses, but less-expensive nylon netting works just as well. Deer simply do not like to put their noses into the netting to eat. The netting can be stretched over the garden, with rocks holding the edges. Use poles strategically located to hold the netting several inches above the plants; if the netting rests on the plants, they will grow through the netting and make harvesting vegetables very difficult. Incidentally, I have also found that this netting generally provides good protection from hail.

Rabbits. Perhaps the number one problem in the Great Plains, rabbits are also the most difficult to deal with. The most effective solution I have found for rabbits as well as the other "big pests" is a sturdy fence and an alert dog or cat, although even this solution is not foolproof. I have had some success with sprinkling a combination of ground black and red pepper on bean plants to prevent rabbits from feeding on young bean flowers (their favorite). The most permanent solution, if they become a serious problem, would be to live-trap the rabbits and transport them into the countryside.

Raccoons. I don't know of any solution that can keep these remarkable creatures from sampling a stand of sweet corn once they have located it, except perhaps a well-constructed electric fence. Some sources suggest spreading moth crystals in your garden, but I think I'd rather have the raccoons. I did notice several years ago in Iowa that they did not like to cross pumpkin patches even to get to corn; apparently they didn't like the scratchy pumpkin leaves. Thus you might discourage them from entering your garden by growing a fence of pumpkins!

Birds. Birds are cute creatures in their place, but not when they pull up young corn plants or eat and pick holes in ripe fruits. Fortunately, the netting used to keep deer out will also work with birds — a relatively inexpensive but very effective solution. Birds also like the seeds in sunflower heads, but they can be discouraged from damaging them by stretching a nylon stocking over the heads as they begin to develop. Several years ago, I had trouble with grackles eating my strawberries through the netting, so I took the advice of a neighbor and gathered a large number of strawberry-sized rocks, which I painted red and spread around my patch. After a few days, the birds quit bothering my strawberries — apparently, picking into a rocky strawberry was not very rewarding!

**Table 5.3
Gardener's Guide
to Vegetable Plant
Problems and
Suggested
Treatments**

Symptom/Problem

A. Leaves with round, white, powdery spots, or coating on leaves and stems (mildews), or masses of small, white flies (whiteflies)

B. Leaves, yellowish or whitish, cottony webs often on bottom (mites, leafhoppers, thrips, red spiders)

C. Holes in leaves (cutworms, weevils, loopers, cabbage worms)

D. Holes in leaves (flea beetles)

E. Holes in leaves (grasshoppers, rhubarb curculio, cutworms)

F. Holes in leaves and fruits (cucumber beetles, bean leaf beetle, Mexican bean beetle)

G. Holes in heads (cutworms)

H. Holes in heads and leaves (pill bugs, slugs, worms)

I. Spots on leaves — round or irregular, often $1/4$ inch or less (leaf spot)

J. Spots on leaves, or irregular with bull's-eyelike rings, spots often $1/2$ inch or so (blight)

K. Leaves folded together (leaf-roller worm)

L. Leaves yellow and die from the bottom up; whole plant eventually dies (fusarium fungi)

M. Leaves stripped of vegetation; fruits often with holes (hornworms)

N. Leaves stripped of vegetation (parsley worms, grasshoppers, asparagus beetles)

O. Leaves chewed on (Colorado potato beetle)

P. Edges of leaves darken (tip burn)

Q. Leaves shrivel and curl, often sticky and shiny below (aphids, psyllids)

R. Leaves curl (physiological)

S. Holes in cobs and leaves (corn earworm, cutworms)

T. Holes in ripe fruit or root (pill bugs, snails)

U. Fruits shriveled and sometimes spotted; plants weak (squash bugs, vine borers)

V. Holes in green fruits (fruitworm, hornworm, pillbugs)

W. Holes in ripe fruit (grasshoppers, crickets, cutworms, June beetle grubs)

X. Leathery spots on fruits (bacterial, fungal, or physiological)

40

Plants Commonly Affected	Treatment
Vine crops, pea, rhubarb, tomato, bean	Bordeaux mixture for fungi; insecticidal soap for flies
Bean, eggplant, tomato, vine crops, potato, pea, others	Insecticidal soap or pyrethrum; spray off with water
Broccoli, cabbage, cauliflower, turnip	Bt for worms; pyrethrum for weevils
Eggplant, radish, broccoli	Rotenone
Rhubarb	Pyrethrum and handpicking
Bean, cucumber, eggplant, sweet potato, others	Rotenone
Cabbage	Bt and handpicking
Lettuce	Bt for worms; handpick slugs or use small dishes of beer to drown them
Tomato	Bordeaux mixture; best to use mulch to prevent spores from splashing from soil to plants; spread plants widely
Tomato, potato	Bordeaux mixture; best to use mulch to prevent spores from splashing soil to plants; spread tomato plants widely
Strawberry	Bt; open leaves and handpick
Tomato	Use resistant varieties; destroy affected plants; spread plants widely
Tomato, potato	Bt or handpick
Asparagus, carrot, dill, parsley	Bt or handpick for worms; pyrethrum and insecticidal soap for grasshoppers and beetles
Potato	Bt or handpick beetles; crush orange eggs and brown larvae; rotenone
Lettuce	Use resistant varieties
Brussels sprout, radish, potato, tomato	Insecticidal soap, pyrethrum
Tomato	Don't overwater; often appears on hot days after cool rainy period
Corn	Bt when silks first appear and every 4 to 5 days thereafter
Pepper, radish, strawberry	Rotenone
Vine crops	Bt for borers; rotenone; sabadilla and pyrethrum for squash bugs and borers
Tomato, squash	Bt or handpick
Tomato	Pyrethrum for grasshoppers; raise fruits off ground for crickets and cutworms
Pepper	Remove affected fruits; treat with Bordeaux mixture

41

Table 5.3 (cont.)

Y. Ripe or green fruits with small green or black spots (bacterial)

Z. Ripe fruits with sunken round spots that often have a dark center (anthracnose fungi)

AA. Ripe fruits with mottled ripening patterns of mixed colors (mosaic virus)

BB. Ripe fruits crack (physiological)

CC. Heads crack (physiological)

DD. Large, dark, soft to leathery spot at the bottom of the fruit (blossom-end rot)

EE. Young plants cut off (cutworm, army cutworm)

FF. Young plants fall over and die (soil fungi — for example, damping-off)

GG. Young plants very weak, slow growing (soil fungi)

HH. Older plants wilt suddenly and often die (bacteria, vine borer)

II. Joints of stem yellowish and weak, leaves with holes (stalk-rot fungi)

JJ. Small to large grayish-white masses on tassels and cobs (smut fungi)

KK. Holes in roots or leaf stalk (carrot weevil)

LL. Tubers or fruits with raised brown areas (bacterial scab)

MM. Margins of leaves curled and brown (leafhopper)

NN. Tubers with holes (wireworms)

OO. Bulbs decayed and tops dead (onion maggot)

Tomato, pepper, cucumber, bean	Bordeaux mixture; mulch and spread plants
Tomato, pepper, cucumber, eggplant	Bordeaux mixture; gather up and destroy old vegetation
Tomato, cucumber	Remove and destroy affected plants
Tomato	Use resistant varieties; don't overwater at ripening stage
Cabbage	Reduce watering
Tomato, pepper	Use resistant varieties; use fertilizer and add calcium to the soil if necessary; often only if the first fruits are affected
Carrot, cole crops, corn, beet, pepper, tomato, others	*Bt*; dig near plant to find and destroy worm
Vine crops	Replant; encourage good drainage
Vine crops	Encourage good drainage
Vine crops	None for bacteria; remove and destroy affected plants; treat with rotenone for insects that transmit the bacteria; for borers, slit stem base and remove borer; sprinkle slit with rotenone
Corn	Use resistant varieties; destroy affected plants
Corn	Remove and destroy affected plants
Carrot, celery	Start *Bt* early and repeat every 4 to 7 days
Cucumber, potato	Bordeaux mixture; try to plant certified seed potatoes; lower soil pH for potatoes
Potato, eggplant	Insecticidal soap and rotenone
Potato	Trap worms in pieces of freshly cut potato
Onion, shallot	Dust bulbs with *Bt* and rotenone when planting; dust plants and soil near plants weekly with *Bt* and rotenone

Chapter Six Weeds

What Is a Weed Anyway? Have you ever wondered what a weed is exactly? Oh, I know everyone recognizes bindweed, pigweed, and foxtail grasses as weeds, or basically undesirable plants, but in parts of my garden, two very desirable plants — asparagus and huckleberry — have become weeds I have to constantly keep in check. How can this be so? First we must look more closely at what defines a weed. Actually, the botanical or agricultural definition of a weed is "any plant that is out of place." Thus foxtail grasses and pigweed are part of the native flora in some areas of the world and as such are not considered weeds. It is only when these plants enter other areas and displace more desirable plants — those in your garden or lawn, for instance — that they disturb our sense of order, and we label them as weeds and rush to jerk them out of the ground. Anyone who has ever made the mistake of planting spearmint in a corner of their garden, and then watched as it rapidly spread, can appreciate how quickly an interesting and attractive herb can become a vicious weed! So a weed — like the asparagus seedlings that popped up everywhere in my garden — is essentially any unwelcome plant!

Weeds are generally either annual or perennial. An annual weed lives only for a single season, during which time it reproduces and spreads by seeds. A perennial weed, by contrast, lives for many seasons and can reproduce itself by seeds or by vegetative means (for example, bulbs and rhizomes). If not controlled, annuals and perennials can be equally aggressive and destructive in a garden.

Achieving Cheap, Permanent Weed Control I have never used a chemical weed killer in my garden. Not only has this saved me money over the years but also it has provided me with peace of mind, because I haven't had to worry about the health effects of these chemicals on my family as we consumed garden produce. I should also tell you that I probably wouldn't garden if I had to spend a great deal of time pulling weeds from my plot — not because I am particularly lazy (I don't believe those articles that tell you how to be a lazy gardener, because I've never known a lazy gardener!) but because I would rather spend the time doing something else equally important but more enjoyable (perhaps fishing).

Through most of the gardening season, and especially during the hot summer months, my garden is essentially weed free. How do I do it? First, I never give weeds a chance to become established. Weeds, like any other plant, develop best only where they receive adequate moisture and nutrients and remain relatively undisturbed. If weeds can't grow to maturity, they won't produce seeds, and they will gradually become less and less abundant in your garden. Even established, tough perennials like bindweed will eventually die if you continually interrupt their growth and drain the energy reserves from their underground parts. Quite simply, I try my hardest to disturb weeds to death. You might think that this sounds like a lot of work, but, actually, the opposite is true. On a 25-by-50-foot garden plot, I spend perhaps 2 or 3 hours each week in the early spring hoeing out weeds; by summer, I spend usually less than 1 hour each week weeding the plot.

Second, the key to eliminating weeds with minimum effort on a

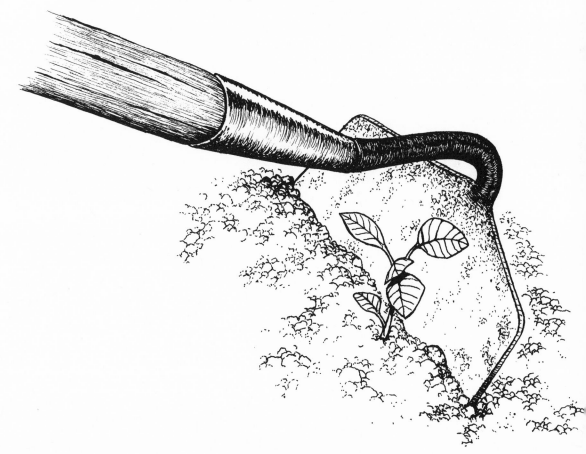

fairly permanent basis in any garden is timing. As soon as the ground warms slightly in the spring, many weed seeds begin to germinate. In many areas of the Great Plains, one of the most pernicious weeds is bindweed. If left unchecked, it will readily overrun a garden plot. Fortunately, in the seedling stage, bindweed and other weeds are extremely vulnerable to simple shallow hoeing. I stroll through the plot and systematically sever or uproot every seedling I notice. Generally, this procedure must be continued for about 2 months (April and May) until the majority of the seeds have germinated. Thereafter, until mid- to late June, whenever I apply a weed-smothering mulch, I simply remain observant and remove the occasional weed seedling that appears. For the rest of the summer, maintaining a neat, weed-free garden is a cinch. Again, I stress that timing is the key. If you wait until mid-June to attack weeds, many will escape by hiding among the foliage of your rapidly developing garden vegetables.

If the Disturbance-Timing Method Doesn't Work

If my disturbance-timing method fails, I erect mechanical barriers. For example, when I gardened in South Dakota, quack grass was a particularly tough problem since it spread rapidly through long, underground stems called rhizomes. Quack grass grew best during cool weather, and it would quickly enter the garden plot from the surrounding lawn in the spring (or in the fall) and crowd out vegetable plants, or at the very least compete with them for moisture and soil nutrients. After futile efforts to control it by handpicking and digging, I finally purchased 12-inch-wide metal flashing (narrower, plastic lawn edging didn't work) at the local lumberyard and buried it around my garden plot, leaving the upper inch exposed. (Bend the edges over since they are relatively sharp.) Result: no more quack grass in my garden. Similar results could probably be obtained by burying 2-by-12-inch redwood boards, but it would be considerably more expensive. The barrier method works equally well in warm regions with bermuda grass, and it should control all vegetatively invasive weeds. The principal disadvantage of underground barriers is that they may slow drainage of the plot, especially in clay soils.

Chapter Seven

Managing Water in Great Plains Gardens

Water is a precious natural resource that in recent years has been the increasing focus (and rightly so) of many conservation efforts. As every gardener knows, water is the lifeblood of the garden and the factor that is most responsible for the general well-being of plants. Even minerals could not nourish plants were water not present to move them throughout the plant body. As we have become more aware of the importance of water, we have also begun to realize that the days when we could take water for granted are gone forever.

In many areas of the Great Plains, especially those where the annual average rainfall may be around 20 inches, water is rarely abundant. Because of this natural scarcity of water, and because of the increasing demands we have made on this limited resource, many communities have passed laws that regulate its use. Watering of lawns and gardens is often permitted only during specified times and for specified periods. You might think that this scarcity of water and these restrictive regulations are limited to areas of the central Great Plains where blazing summers and searing winds are common. This is not the case. While gardening in Colorado Springs, in the foothills of the Rocky Mountains, I was once subjected to restrictions that allowed watering only every other day for 4 hours.

During a severe drought in west-central Kansas, I heard some people comment that they were not even going to put a garden out. After all, I overheard one explain, "if you can only water once a week for three hours, what's the use?" Although such restrictive watering regulations may discourage folks from gardening, it doesn't have to be that way. The following techniques and tools will enable you to have a thriving vegetable patch while doing your part to conserve water even under severe restrictions.

¶ Use soaker hoses. These rubber or canvas hoses leak water slowly from their surface. They can either be buried or be laid on top of the soil all season. I prefer to keep mine above ground (covered with mulch) since they must be taken up for fall tilling.

¶ Use drip irrigation. These systems of narrow plastic emitters or tubes with small holes drip water directly at the base of the plant. As with soaker hoses, they can be placed above or below ground.

¶ Don't use overhead sprinklers. Sprinklers allow an excessive amount of water to evaporate without ever reaching the soil. Besides, if the watering restrictions in your community permit watering only in the evening (as is often the case), allowing the plant leaves to be wet overnight from sprinkling encourages fungal diseases.

¶ Deep soak your plants. By using soaker hoses or bubblers that fit on the end of a hose to deep soak your soil, you can encourage plants to develop deep-seated root systems that will enable them to better withstand drought. If you use trenches along with bubblers and mulch, you can effectively deep soak your garden as well as minimize water losses due to evaporation.

¶ Use mulches. Mulches are extremely effective in preventing loss of water from the soil surface. Try this experiment. Take two ordinary sponges and soak them in water. Lay one of them on the surface of your garden without any protection; lay the other on the surface of your garden and cover it with 4 or 5 inches of straw or grass or a layer of plastic. See how long it takes each sponge to dry out. (Don't sit and watch the one under the mulch — you may be there for several days.) Even under extreme water restrictions, you can have a garden if you use soaker hoses or drip irrigation under mulches. Read chapter 4 ("Mulches") for more information.

¶ Water in the evening or at night. Watering during this time of the day will minimize water losses due to evaporation.

¶ Provide windbreaks. Consider erecting a fence to break the wind flow across your garden and to slow evaporation from plant leaves. Alternatively, you can plant your tall crops (for example, corn and asparagus) so they serve as a fence.

¶ Avoid raised beds. In warm, windy areas, raised beds dry out more quickly than level ones; unless you have poor drainage or want the beds to warm up quickly in the early spring, don't use them.

¶ Influence politicians. Educate community officials to such water-conserving ideas as soaker hoses and encourage them to set appropriate priorities when developing watering restrictions. Surely, the less fortunate family using soaker hoses to raise a vegetable garden to supplement their food supply ought to have priority in watering over someone using a sprinkler to keep a lawn green. Suggest that procedures be developed so that perhaps gardeners could apply for a permit to water at additional times if they are using methods such as drip irrigation under mulch.

Chapter Eight

Gardening in the Wind

When I moved to Rhode Island at the age of twenty-one after having lived in Kansas for the previous nineteen years, it was quite a shock. It really bothered me that I could not see to the horizon over unbroken prairie, that the population was denser, and that the countryside was more developed than in my state. At the same time, I was fascinated by the beauty of the deciduous woods and inspired by the gorgeous display of fall colors. However, I also remember something else about that first year, something that was different and somewhat confusing. When it snowed, the snow fell straight down! As a youngster, I had never seen snow that was not accompanied by wind. I thought snow came down sideways!

Not all areas of the Great Plains have major problems with wind. However, in a significant portion of the central United States, the days without wind are often the most noticeable. During the spring and summer, the wind is especially variable, and whether you garden or fish, paint or build houses, you have to plan for it. If you don't, you'll be frequently disappointed and even more frequently frustrated. You'll probably never learn to like the wind, but if you learn to live, and to garden, with it, you'll hardly notice it — most of the time.

Wind in the Heartland comes in different forms. During storms, it arrives suddenly, often accompanied by hail, and may exert its fury for 10 to 30 minutes at speeds of 30 to 60 or more miles an hour. These winds tend to do rapid damage to plants and test the immediate resiliency of both the gardener and the garden. At other times, as, for example, during the period when late spring is changing to summer, the wind sometimes blows, day and night, for 2 or 3 days. Although the wind's speed is usually only 10 to 25 miles an hour, it is persistent and can effectively drain the energy from garden and gardener alike. Finally, summer days often begin with a light breeze that develops into a hot (90° to 100°F), 15-to-25-mile-an-hour wind, which gradually calms as the sun sets. Regardless of the type of wind, the Heartland gardener must prepare for it.

Protecting Your Garden from the Wind

In order to live with the wind in your garden, remember first that you'll never be able to beat it, so in your planning make sure that you consider the effect of wind on whatever you do. The seven-foot-tall trellises of pole beans that you see in those lush green gardens on television gardening programs are simply not realistic in areas where wind is a significant factor. Here are a few suggestions to help you learn to live with the wind in your garden.

¶ Use Wallo'Waters or hotkaps. Young transplants are especially vulnerable to wind damage. Not only will the wind frequently twist or break leaves off the plant and cause extra water stress by increased evaporation, but it will often break the plant off at the ground. Wallo'Waters and hotkaps prevent this by protecting plants from the wind. Wallo'Waters are sturdier than hotkaps, however, and so are superior, particularly in areas subject to sustained or high winds. Since during storms winds are often accompanied by rain or hail, Wallo'Waters offer additional protection that waxed-paper hotkaps are unable to provide. Furthermore, if you use hotkaps, you must anchor the edges firmly with soil to prevent them from being blown away during high winds.

¶ Throw out those conical tomato cages, or at least limit their use to smaller plants such as peppers. Even then anchor them securely. Their inverted conical shape makes them very unstable when they are subjected to strong winds, especially if they are supporting a large tomato plant. Even when anchored with stakes, these cages commonly blow over during wind- and rainstorms when the ground is saturated. The best supports in wind that I have used are large round cages composed of rectangular wire mesh with openings several inches wide. Don't use the concrete reinforcing gage wire, because it is difficult to bend; rather, use a lighter gage that is easily worked with your hands. The cages should be constructed so their diameter is 2 to 2½ feet. Anchor the cages by driving four 5-foot-long light metal (the plastic-coated ones are great), bamboo, or wooden poles at least 18 inches into the ground, evenly spacing each one around the cage. The poles should then be attached to the cage with twist ties. The cage must be strong enough to support the mature plant but resilient enough to bend in the wind. Resiliency is important to keep in mind because when winds are really

high, a rigid structure is more liable to be damaged. Large plastic garbage sacks can be placed around the cage to create a hotkap effect for the young plant. The main disadvantage of these cages is storage — they take up a considerable amount of space. I have also had success with square collapsible cages, made from heavy gauge wire. Anchor them as with the round cages; then wrap plastic or place Wallo'Water (left) around the bottom of each cage to protect the young transplant from the wind. One big advantage of collapsible cages is that they are easy to store — 8 to 10 will stand or lie flat in a relatively small area.

¶ Time your watering. Don't soak the ground immediately before or during periods of high wind. This often results in the plant being blown over since the roots have difficulty anchoring the plant in the soggy ground. Plants with large leaves and shallow root systems, such as broccoli, are especially vulnerable.

¶ Select wind-resistant varieties. You may never have thought about it, but some plant varieties are more resistant to wind than others. For instance, with broccoli I have found that the shorter, stockier varieties do better in the wind. Thus Packman works out much better than the taller Green Duke. Similarly, certain varieties of peas (for example, Oregon Sugar Pod and Little Marvel) withstand the wind much better than others (for example, Thomas Laxton). Experiment with different varieties to determine their wind resistance.

¶ Grow living windbreaks. When planting your garden, try to plan for the wind. Decide which direction the wind comes from most of the time, and plant sturdier, taller varieties such as corn to take the brunt of the wind and protect weaker crops such as beans and tomatoes. Don't worry if the corn blows over in a strong wind; it will recover quickly. I have also planted asparagus in my garden to help break the wind. Once established, these sturdy plants can take considerable wind — mine have suffered 80-to-90-mile-an-hour winds without perishing.

¶ Avoid rigid trellises. Don't grow vegetables like cucumbers up trellises attached to rigid structures such as fences, because these structures do not give sufficiently (sway enough) during high winds. As a result, trellises attached to such structures are also generally not resilient enough in winds, and the vines are often severely damaged or torn from them. I grow my cucumbers either on the ground behind living wind-breaks or up medium-height (4 to 5 feet) trellises constructed of lighter gage wire. I then anchor the trellises with light metal, bamboo, or wooden poles driven into the ground and attached to each trellis with twist ties. Even in 50-mile-an-hour winds, these trellises have not blown over, although they have swayed severely.

¶ Consider using floating row covers. These products are light fabric or fabriclike materials that can be draped over plants for protection. They allow light and water to reach plants but provide protection from wind, frost, and insects. The edges must be secured with boards or they will blow away during high winds.

¶ Use mulches. Wind has a tremendous drying effect on the soil, and mulches can significantly reduce water loss from evaporation of soil moisture into the atmosphere (see chapter 4 for more information on mulches).

¶ Use soaking methods for watering. As a rule, I do not recommend overhead watering to any gardener since it encourages leaf diseases. But in windy areas there is an additional reason not to overhead water with sprinklers: evaporation. Use soaker hoses or bubblers that fit on the ends of hoses for soaking. Regulate the water flow so that there is no runoff; the object is to soak the ground so it will stay moist until the next soaking. If you use a combination of soaking and mulches, you should have to water your garden only once or twice a week during even the worst dry spells. Soaking methods and mulches should save you at least 30 to 50 percent on your water bill.

Chapter Nine **Is There Garden Life after a Hailstorm?**

Gardeners who have experienced severe weather, especially in the Great Plains, recognize and dread the signs: a rapidly moving, turbulent, greenish-gray cloud front preceded by a sharp drop in temperature. Usually these conditions indicate that a hailstorm is approaching, although the severity of the hail associated with such storms is always unknown. With any luck, the hail is brief and causes little damage, but all too often it seems to wreak havoc on the nearest garden — usually yours! As disheartening as it is to see a carefully tended and robust garden abruptly destroyed, the gardener certainly should not quit for the season. Why? Because the most destructive hailstorms often occur early enough in the season that many vegetables can be replanted and grown to maturity. In addition, some vegetable plants, even though damaged, can be coaxed back into full production with a little effort. Finally, gardeners are simply not the type of people to let a hailstorm put an end to a full season's gardening. If your garden has been the victim of a severe hailstorm, this guide should help you to revitalize your patch.
¶ Wait. Don't do anything in your garden for 2 or 3 days. Since the most damaging hailstorms are usually accompanied by heavy rains that saturate the soil, waiting allows the ground to drain sufficiently to lessen the risk of damaging the soil by packing during subsequent revitaliza-

**Map 9.1
Average dates
of the last killing
frost in spring**

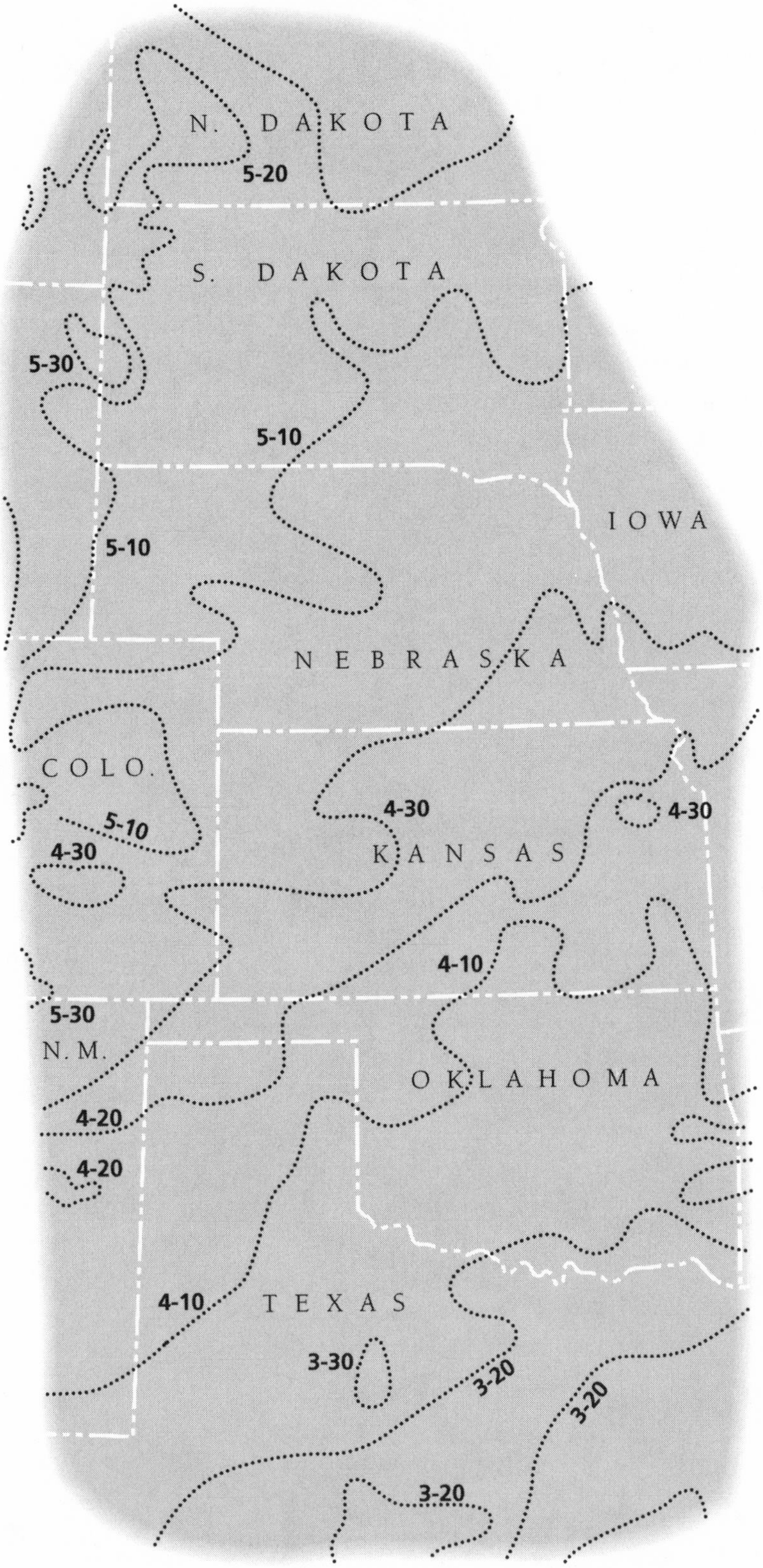

N. DAKOTA
5-20

S. DAKOTA

5-30

5-10

5-10

IOWA

NEBRASKA

COLO.
5-10
4-30

4-30

4-30

KANSAS

4-10

5-30
N.M.

OKLAHOMA

4-20

4-20

4-10

TEXAS

3-30

3-20

3-20

3-20

Map 9.2
Average dates
of the first killing
frost in fall

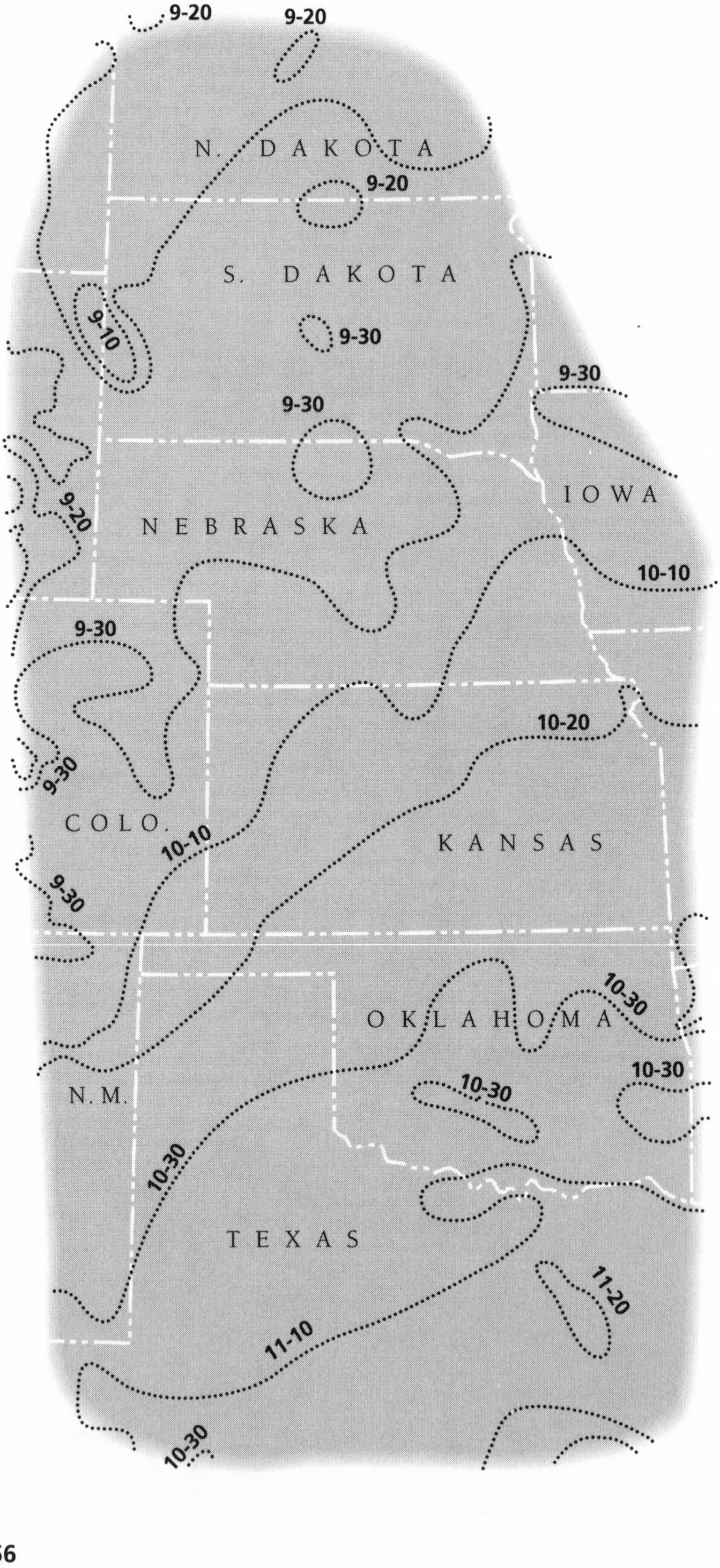

9-20   9-20

N. DAKOTA
9-20

S. DAKOTA
9-30

9-10

9-30

9-30

IOWA

9-20

NEBRASKA

10-10

9-30

10-20

9-30

COLO.

10-10

KANSAS

9-30

10-30

OKLAHOMA

N.M.

10-30

10-30

10-30

10-30

TEXAS

11-20

10-30

11-10

10-30

tion. Use this period to consult Map 9.2, which shows first fall frost dates, to determine which vegetables are likely to produce a harvest if replanted. Perhaps more important, waiting allows the impact of losing the garden to diminish and the planting urge characteristic of all gardeners to resurface.

¶ Evaluate and revitalize. During this phase, you will be setting the stage for bringing your garden back to its former lush condition, and the decisions you make will determine your ultimate success. Examine your vegetables closely and decide which will need to be replanted and which can be salvaged. Some plants (for example, tomatoes) have the ability to recover from even severe damage, but the way these damaged plants are tended will determine how well they respond. The methods and treatments that I have found successful with different vegetables during revitalization are outlined in "How to Treat Hail-Damaged Plants" at the end of this section.

¶ Follow some general revitalization dos and don'ts. First, after salvaging any plant, apply a complete, water-soluble fertilizer, such as Miracle-Gro, around the base of each one. Most plants also benefit from a light dusting of *Bt* and rotenone, since damaged plants are especially inviting to insects. Don't throw damaged plants in your compost pile, because it seems to encourage diseases and insects. Finally, avoid the temptation to retill your garden prior to planting lest you wreck your garden's soil structure.

¶ Experiment. When in doubt, experiment. After a punishing hailstorm in my Kansas garden in late June 1984 (15 minutes of inch-size hailstones driven by 70-to-90-mile-an-hour winds), I was given skeptical-to-downright-negative opinions about whether replanted corn would make a harvest in the shortened growing season that remained. However, our family loves to eat fresh roasting ears, so after consulting a first fall-frost date for our region, I planted three varieties, a short season (Burpee Sunglow), a middle season (Jubilee), and a long season (Silver Queen). To our delight, the middle and late varieties provided us with a wonderful late-season picking of fresh corn. Unless there is absolutely no possibility that a vegetable will reach harvest, you have everything to gain and little to lose by replanting.

¶ Keep records. Get a notebook and jot down the results of your revitalization efforts. By recording the methods and varieties that were successful, you will have valuable information to use in any subsequent garden rescues you might have to conduct.

¶ Enjoy. Revitalizing a garden can be a lot of work. However, you'll be amazed at the recuperative abilities of many plants, and the best part is you'll have the pleasure of eating the results. Is there garden life after a hailstorm? You bet there is!

Table 9.1 How to Treat Hail-Damaged Plants

Vegetable	Treatment	Comments
Asparagus, rhubarb, strawberries, and other perennials	Trim dead stems and leaves	Perennial plants recover marvelously after a storm; they are exciting to watch!
Beans	Replant	Leave roots of plants in soil during revitalization to provide extra nitrogen
Beets, carrots, and other root crops	Trim severely damaged tops and dust plants lightly with rotenone	Most root crops recover rapidly and strongly
Cole crops	Treat for insects with *Bt* and rotenone; by removing damaged heads or shoots, side heads or shoots will develop	Broccoli and cabbage recover well
Corn	Replant if time permits	Damaged plants usually produce a poor yield and are subject to disease
Cucumbers and other melons	May recover if trimmed; replant if long growing season remains	
Peppers	Trim dead leaves and stems; transplant if plants are available	Recover slowly if at all
Potatoes	Trim dead stems	Plant quick-recovery varieties if your area has a lot of hailstorms
Squash	Trim dead stems and leaves	Recover well if any healthy stems remain
Tomatoes	Trim to the main stem and a couple of strong laterals; remove damaged fruit	Superb plants for rejuvenating the spirit; recover quickly and strongly!

Chapter Ten # The Farmers' Market: Sharing the Bounty

If you become involved in gardening to any extent, you'll quickly learn how productive well-cared-for plants can become. In fact, they can make rabbits look lazy by comparison! So what do you do with the surplus? If you're like me you give to neighbors, friends, and relatives. But then what? Let me make a suggestion: Use a farmers' market as an outlet. What is a farmers' market? In the simplest terms, it is a place where the consumer can purchase garden products directly from the local producer without middle-level salespeople. Our market was organized by our county extension agent, who also serves as the market manager. It meets each Saturday morning during the summer in the local courthouse parking lot.

The principal objectives of most farmers' markets are the same as those outlined for the farmers' market in my area. First, they provide a place where the home gardener can sell directly to the consumer; second, they permit high-quality, locally produced vegetables to be available to local consumers; third, they encourage local participation in the marketing of the vegetables; last, they encourage the increased production of locally grown vegetables for local consumption.

The benefits of a local farmers' market are many. Not only can you, the home gardener, sell your excess produce, but consumers can enjoy products that are generally superior to those found at the same time in local supermarkets. You may even make a profit on your produce. In any event, I'll guarantee you'll meet a great group of fellow gardeners and people anxious to buy fresh, quality vegetables. You'll find yourself looking forward to Saturday morning, or whenever the market meets, as a pleasant social event. Whether you sell only occasionally or decide to get serious and make money at a farmers' market, the following tips will help you increase your chances for success.

¶ Visit a farmers' market and learn the rules. For example, normally only local growers and producers may sell at a farmers' market, that is, out of state producers are usually restricted.

¶ If there is no farmers' market in your area encourage your local horticultural/agricultural extension official to develop one. If there isn't an extension agent in your area, get together with several local gardeners and establish your own farmers' market. Be sure you are aware of local ordinances and state laws regarding the sale of produce. Often, processed products, such as honey, require state health certification before they may be sold.

¶ Learn which vegetables are most in demand and, especially, when. You might easily be able to sell 100 pounds of tomatoes for a dollar per pound early in the season but have trouble selling them for 40 cents per pound in the middle of the summer when almost everyone has a relative with excess fruits. On the other hand, some vegetables, such as onions, are usually in demand throughout the season.

¶ Try to be the earliest producer with vegetables like tomatoes, because you'll receive premium prices for your produce. Use devices such as Wallo'Waters to give your plants an extra-early start.

¶ Stagger your plantings of each vegetable so that your harvest will not be concentrated into one short period. For example, by planting beans every 10 days from late spring through midsummer, you can insure your customers of a continual supply of this vegetable. Experiment with other vegetables to see how you can stretch their harvest periods.

¶ Sell only fresh, quality produce. You'll have lots of competition, so your produce should look and be the best. If the eggplant someone bought from you was the greatest they've ever had, they'll remember you and come back; if not, you've seen the last of them.

¶ If you don't use any pesticides or fungicides on your vegetables or perhaps use only natural types, don't hesitate to emphasize this point. I found that many people prefer to buy produce treated with natural compounds rather than with synthetics.

Chapter Eleven

Vegetable Lineup

Asparagus Asparagus is an exciting vegetable. Not only is it the first vegetable to be harvested in quantity in the spring, it also tastes fantastic! In addition, it reappears year after year with relatively little maintenance, it is extremely productive, and it looks graceful in the garden. I am convinced that asparagus can be grown almost anywhere. As an experiment, I planted a patch several years ago in a poorly prepared clay soil, and recently it produced a nice crop of asparagus — despite being subjected to intense heat (110°F) and cold (-25°F), vicious winds (70–80 MPH), hail (golfball size), and poor drainage (water from melting snow remained for 5 to 7 days). Asparagus is tough!

Growing Essentials
The First Year

¶ Loosen the soil to a depth of at least 12 to 18 inches either by hand digging or with a rototiller. Add 4 to 8 cubic feet of compressed peat to each 10-by-10-foot plot and work in thoroughly. I use compressed peat because I want to make sure no weeds (for example, bindweed) are introduced at this step. Remember that asparagus is a perennial that will live for many years, and you must prepare the soil accordingly — don't cheat on the amount of organic matter.

¶ Spread at least 4 pounds of a 20–4–8, 27–3–3, or similar high-nitrogen fertilizer on the prepared bed and work it into the top 6 to 8 inches. This is necessary because the high level of organic matter in the soil will encourage increased microbial activity that will rapidly deplete nitrogen levels.

¶ You might start your own plants, but I suggest that you get your roots either from a local greenhouse or a mail-order firm. Be sure they are certified disease-free. I have used one- and two-year-old roots and have had excellent results with both, rarely losing a plant. If anything, the

61

two-year-old plants seem to take longer to sprout when planted. It is essential that the roots are healthy; avoid roots that are moldy, a sure sign of poor storage. Look for roots that do not appear to be dried out or that have long sprouts growing from them. The roots should be fleshy and relatively stiff, not shriveled.

New, disease-resistant strains of hybrid asparagus are now available, as well as a new hybrid, all-male strain that, according to one seed and nursery catalog, "doubles, triples, sometimes quadruples the yields of older varieties." This increased production is because the male plants do not have to waste any energy producing flowers and fruits. Although I am trying some of these newer varieties in my garden, my main crop variety remains the old standard, Mary Washington. Curiously, in my own patches over the years, most of the male plants have died, and 85 percent or more of the remaining plants are female.

¶ You can plant your asparagus bed anytime in the spring from 4 weeks before the last average frost date up to 2 weeks after it. For example, in central Kansas, which has an average last-frost date of April 20, I planted asparagus patches on March 20, April 10, and May 1, whereas in western South Dakota, I planted my patch on May 15. All of the patches did well. Keep in mind that hard freezes will kill asparagus shoots that are above the ground, so don't be surprised if this happens should you plant early. Even when this happened to me, I never had a root that didn't survive and produce more shoots.

¶ Dig a trench in the prepared plot 8 inches deep and about 10 inches wide at the bottom. Cover the bottom ¼ inch deep with a 14–28–14, 12–22–6, or similar fertilizer. Cover this with 1 inch of compressed peat and then 1 inch of soil. You are now ready for your plants.

¶ Contrary to much published information, I have not found that asparagus plants need to be planted several feet apart. I plant mine 12 inches apart in rows 2 feet apart and have had great results. Planting asparagus plants this close saves space and also discourages weeds from growing beneath them. A 10-by-30-foot area with 75 plants will provide all of the asparagus a family of five could possibly use.

¶ Place your plants in the trench with the raised crown portion pointed up and spread the roots the width of the trench. Cover the roots first with 2 inches of soil and then with 1 inch of compressed peat. The final layer of compressed peat will help keep the soil surface from drying out too quickly. Thoroughly soak each trench, being careful not to wash away the compressed peat.

¶ Shoots should appear above ground in about 8 to 30 days, depending on how warm the ground is and how long it has been since your roots were harvested for sale. The fresher they are, the more quickly they will sprout.

¶ Be sure to keep the plants watered while they are establishing themselves the first summer.

¶ The shoots will grow into a dense "fern" stage that is the aboveground part of the asparagus plant. Do not remove any of this, because it is the part of the plant that is manufacturing foods that will be stored in the roots. These stored foods will be the source of energy for the plant when it begins to produce shoots the next spring. A good supply of stored foods insures that many shoots will be produced for you to eat.

¶ Leave the top growth on the plants until it is thoroughly dead from frosts; remove and destroy it in late winter (that is, mid-January to February). This eliminates hiding places for potential pests and allows for easier shoot harvesting in the spring.

The Second Year

¶ Unless snowfall or rainfall has been above average, thoroughly soak your patch several times in the early spring beginning at least 6 to 8 weeks before the last frost. Deep soak every 4 to 8 days until shoots begin to appear and then every 10 days or so, depending on the weather. I have found that asparagus plants deprived of water early in the season produce poorly.

¶ When the first shoot appears, fertilize each 10-by-10-foot plot with 4

63

to 5 pounds of an 8–10–8 (or equivalent) fertilizer and rake the soil lightly (1 inch deep).

¶ After a dozen or so shoots appear, harvest those and all shoots that appear during the next 4 weeks. Some books recommend not harvesting the second year, but my own experience and research indicate that harvesting the second year encourages the roots to spread.

¶ Following the harvest period, fertilize with a water-soluble fertilizer and then twice again at mid- and late summer.

The Third and Following Years
Follow the steps given for the second year but harvest for 6 to 8 weeks.

Pests and Diseases

Insects that most often bother asparagus are asparagus beetles and grasshoppers. Both can be controlled with applications of pyrethrum and rotenone, but, remember, pyrethrum also kills beneficial insects. Aphids are sometimes a serious problem but can be treated effectively with insecticidal soap. Asparagus rust, a fungal disease, can usually be avoided by planting rust-resistant varieties. Another fungal disease, crown rot, causes spindly, yellowish plants, and I am careful to dig up and discard such plants when I see them.

Storing

Asparagus will keep for several weeks in the refrigerator if the bases of the spears are kept in fresh water. We also preserve spears by freezing, but they do not retain the crisp nature of fresh spears. In preparation for freezing, we trim the ends, wash the spears thoroughly, and place them in boiling water for 3 minutes. We then plunge them into cold tap water until they are cool and package them in plastic sacks.

Next to grasses, beans are the most important food crop on earth,

Asparagus Varieties I Have Tested (my favorite,*)

Mary Washington*	My main crop variety; excellent production

I also have Brock's Imperial, Robert's Giant, and Waltham growing in my Kansas garden.

Beans providing a rich source of protein for millions of people. Grown worldwide, this wonderful vegetable is apparently native to tropical South America, where wild varieties still exist. Beans are important in the home garden because they are delicious and they store well. Boiled with a strip of bacon and a shallot or two, nothing tastes better at a meal in late July or during a snowstorm in February than a pot of fresh or preserved snap beans. And nothing reminds me more of the pleasures of gardening.

Although there are several types of beans found in home gardens, I would venture to say that the most popular is the green snap bean. They are easy to grow (either as bush or pole varieties), nearly all are stringless, and they tolerate a wide range of soil conditions (except wet). Despite being subject to numerous pests and diseases, snap beans grow and produce a crop so fast that a first picking is almost assured.

Growing Essentials

¶ Select a sunny spot with silty or sandy loam soil. Even though beans are not heavy users of soil minerals, prior to planting I always mix in a granular fertilizer (for example, 8–10–8) at a rate of 2 pounds in each 10-by-10-foot area. Avoid high-nitrogen fertilizers, because pod production might be reduced.

¶ Plant beans about 1 inch deep and 1 to 2 inches apart and cover them firmly with soil. Rows should be about 18 inches apart for easy harvesting. Water them thoroughly after planting. Beans should begin to appear in about 7 to 10 days. Don't worry if you have clayey soils and

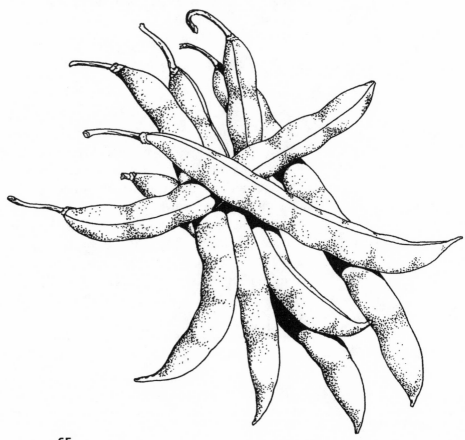

the beans appear to struggle through the soil crust — they always make it.

¶ Beans can be planted almost anytime from late spring through mid-July, but our best luck has always been with crops planted between May 1 (in warmer areas like Kansas) to June 1 (in cooler areas like the Black Hills of South Dakota). If you want to take a chance, plant some earlier (for instance, in mid-April), but remember, even light frosts will often kill beans. In the Great Plains, you can begin to pick beans in earnest about 45 to 60 days after putting seeds into the ground.

Pests and Diseases

The pests I have had the most serious problems with are mites, cucumber beetles, Mexican bean beetles, and bean leaf beetles. Mites are especially troublesome during hot weather, but by early planting and harvesting they can usually be avoided. However, when I planted a late crop and had a problem, I had some success applying an insecticidal soap, if I recognized the infestation soon enough. If this pest cannot be controlled, be sure to remove and destroy severely infested plants. Various beetles that eat holes in the leaves and pods can be easily controlled with a dusting of rotenone. With their preference for bean flowers, rabbits can be an especially serious problem in a bean patch. The best protection I have found is a well-maintained fence and an alert dog or cat.

Storing

Although snap beans can be preserved by canning, they seem to lose much of their garden-fresh flavor. Our favorite way to preserve them is by freezing, but you must be careful to prepare them properly or they will develop a strong flavor in storage. We snap the ends off, wash the pods thoroughly, and then blanch them by boiling them in water for 3 minutes. Blanching destroys the enzymes in beans, or any other vegetable, that might cause a strong taste to develop in storage. They can be french cut prior to blanching. After we boil the beans, we then plunge them into cold tap water until they are cool. Finally, we package them in 1-pound units in plastic freezer bags and freeze them. Prepared and stored this way, snap beans taste fresh well into the spring.

Bean Varieties I Have Tested (my favorite,*; B, bush; P, pole)

Bush Blue Lake*,B	Excellent overall; heavy producer of long, flat pods; excellent flavor and freezes well; stems are fairly brittle and break easily during harvesting; later than Spartan Arrow
Green Crop*,B	Excellent overall; produces heavily and provides an especially heavy second picking; excellent flavor and freezes well

66

Spartan Arrow[*,B]	Excellent overall; heavy producer of long, round, tender pods; in my opinion, this has the best flavor; freezes well
Tendercrop[*,B]	Excellent overall; produces heavily and provides an especially heavy second picking; excellent flavor and freezes well

Others I have tried include Green Isle[B], Greenpod[B], Kentucky Wonder[B,P], Shamrock[B], and Yellow Wax[B].

Beets I doubt there is any other vegetable that, when properly prepared, rivals the beet in taste. One of our favorite ways to prepare them is to boil, peel, and quarter several fresh, young beets (about lemon size), place them in the microwave for several minutes in a covered dish with several pats of butter and a squirt of lemon juice, and then eat them piping hot. Served this way, even my eight-year-old son, Scotty, thinks they are great and refers to them as "candied beets."

Growing Essentials
¶ Beets are relatively easy to grow when the ground has been properly prepared. Although not especially picky about soil, they do best in a loamy, fertile location with plenty of sunlight. Beets are very tolerant of both hot and cold weather.

¶ Beets are sometimes erratic in germination, so I always use fresh seeds. Beet seeds in the 3- or 9-cent packages that you often find in chain stores in the spring will produce just as good a crop as seeds in the more expensive packages, providing the variety is the same.

¶ Beets are a root crop and benefit especially from phosphorus in the development of the root system. Consequently, when preparing the ground for my beets, I usually add 0–20–0 and 8–10–8 fertilizers at a rate of 1½ pounds each in a 10-by-10-foot area.

¶ To insure that my seeds germinate in the early spring, I dig a trench about ½ inch deep, place my seeds in the trench, cover them with a good potting soil, water them thoroughly, and then cover the entire row with a plastic wrap, securing the edges with boards. This warms the soil and also keeps it moist. Seedlings will usually emerge within 5 to 7 days. Allow 12 inches between rows.

¶ Beets don't require much attention, and given adequate moisture they will thrive. However, I have learned over the years that to produce a good crop of roots, they must be thinned to about 1½ to 3 inches apart, preferably when the seedlings are about 1 inch tall. Don't be fooled by the large size of the tops in unthinned beets; most of the roots will remain small. Beets are usually ready to eat (lemon to orange size) in 8 to 10 weeks.

67

Did You Know?
Plant Hairs

The Beautiful

Have you ever wondered why a bean leaf clings to you as you harvest beans? Or what causes the scratchy feeling on a pumpkin leaf that raccoons and deer find so irritating? Or why petunia and snapdragon flowers are so sticky? If you have looked closely, you probably have noticed that many plant surfaces appear to be covered by hairs and that they differ from plant to plant and sometimes from one part of the plant to another. Although the hairs are often so small that they probably appear rather uninteresting to the unaided eye, they are actually one of the most remarkable features of plants.

You might guess that the assortment of hairs found on the leaf must serve some function for the plant, and you would be right. In fact, many plants would have a difficult time surviving were it not for such hairs. Why? Remember that plants, unlike animals, are not mobile and must contend with the environment in which they grow. Plants can't run and hide from predators or find a cool shady spot on a hot summer day. They must stand and fight the elements, including hungry grasshoppers, high winds, sap-sucking aphids, searing temperatures, to name only a few. To survive against such negative influences, plants must develop defenses, and plant hairs are one of the first lines of this defense.

How do the hairs work, and what do they defend against? Glandular hairs, such as those found on petunias and snapdragons, excrete sticky fluids that are uncomfortable and distasteful to many insects and thus discourage them from chewing or sucking on these plants. Insects like the grasshopper, for instance, are often discouraged from eating plants in the squash family because of their sharp, rigid hairs. Pointed or hooked hairs not only prevent damage from hungry insects but also kill such soft-bodied pests as aphids by literally puncturing their body wall and causing loss of fluids. In addition to protecting a plant from insects or animals, hairs can prevent loss of water from leaves by providing a covering that slows the wind down as it crosses the leaf surface; as a result, less water is lost from the plant's breathing pores (stomata) through evaporation. This is especially true with plants that have a thick layer of long hairs, such as the raspberry. But even plants without this type of hair covering benefit to at least some degree — for example, the eggplant, with its elaborate branched, star-shaped hairs. Finally, some plants, such as the tomato, have hairs that produce substances that repel insects as well as prevent loss of water. Truly, the microscopic world of plant hairs is a place of marvels!

The Practical

While working in your garden, remember these things about plant hairs.

¶ The purpose of some pointed hairs is to irritate the skin by breaking the surface and sometimes injecting foreign substances. If you are bothered by rashes when working with plants such as pumpkins, wear light gloves and long sleeves.

¶ Hairs are often very effective at holding moisture next to the surface of the plant. Thus, if you sprinkle your plants late in the evening, the leaf surface may remain excessively wet for long periods of time, and this will often encourage the growth of some fungi. If at all possible, do not wet densely hairy leaf surfaces, especially during warm weather.

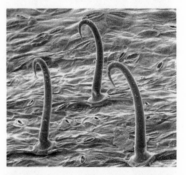

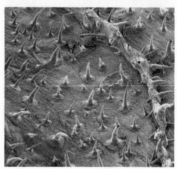

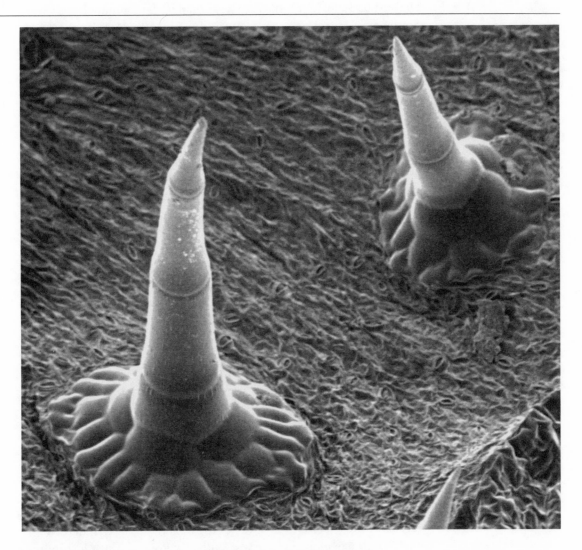

The variety of hairs found on leaves is astounding. The elongate, ropelike features (upper left) on the surface are leaf veins, which carry food and water throughout the plant. Frequently, pests seek out the veins and puncture them to extract cell sap, thereby damaging the plant. Hairs help protect the plant from such damage. Those of beans (upper left, magnified 36 times and middle left, magnified 110 times) and squash (lower left, magnified 36 times and above, magnified 360 times) illustrate their structural and functional beauty. The hook-shaped hairs on beans and the massive and sharply pointed ones on squash also explain why bean leaves cling to your clothes during harvest and why squash leaves feel rough and scratchy.

69

Pests and Diseases

I haven't had a lot of trouble with pests on my beets, although cutworms can cause serious damage to seedlings during the first few weeks. If you dig in the soil immediately around a recently damaged seedling, you can usually find the culprit and destroy it; in serious infestations, they can be eliminated with *Bt*. Incidentally, I have found that grasshoppers like to hide in beet greens, although they do not seem to eat them. Diseases that may attack beets include leaf spots (fungus), heart and root rots (bacteria), and scab (the same one on potatoes), but I have rarely lost a beet to any of these. Good garden sanitation and proper watering techniques (for example, not splashing soil on the plants or keeping the soil wet) should help to prevent these diseases.

Storing

Beets store readily providing the temperature is cool enough and they can be kept from drying out. I prepare them by washing off the dirt and removing all but about $1/2$ to 1 inch of the tops; don't remove any of the bottom. Dry the surface of the beets thoroughly and then store them in a sealed plastic container in a refrigerator at 40° to 50°F. Stored this way, beets will keep from 3 to 6 weeks.

Beet Varieties I Have Tested (my favorite,*)

Detroit Dark Red*	Excellent overall; produces a great crop of early midseason beets and can be left to grow to neighbor-impressing size (4 to 5 pounds)
Early Wonder	Produces a nice crop of beets but is not as vigorous as Detroit Dark Red

Broccoli, Brussels Sprouts, Cabbage, and Cauliflower

It might surprise you that broccoli, brussels sprouts, cabbage, and cauliflower all belong to a single species called *Brassica oleracea*. These vegetables are referred to as the cole crops, a term derived from their medieval designation as coleworts. With cabbage and brussels sprouts, we actually eat mostly leaves, but with cauliflower and broccoli, the portion we prize is the flowering head. It is reported that eating certain cole crops (for example, broccoli) might help protect a person against such diseases as cancer.

Broccoli

I'm always surprised when people who visit my garden in west-central Kansas express disbelief at the lush broccoli plants they see. After all, they had always heard and read that broccoli is a cool-season plant, and the Heartland is certainly not noted for its cool summer temperatures.

Yet I can tell them honestly that broccoli is one of the easiest vegetables to grow and that I sometimes have more problems growing tomatoes. The secret to growing consistently huge crops of broccoli, especially in warm-weather areas, is timing. Broccoli is a cool-season crop, and for it to develop to its fullest potential, it must do the majority of its growth in the early-through-late-spring period when daytime temperatures usually do not exceed 80°F. Broccoli, like all cole crops, is very resistant to the cold. In the Great Plains, most of the failures I have seen in growing broccoli resulted from planting too late.

Growing Essentials

¶ Select the best variety. There is absolutely no doubt that the variety you choose can determine your success in growing this vegetable. For example, in South Dakota I simply could not get Waltham 29 to grow for me, whereas Green Comet flourished. I have learned that the differences among varieties in the size, weight, and shape of heads, the uniformity of harvest dates, the development of side heads, and the overall plant height are as pronounced as night and day.

¶ Start plants 7 (13, for extra-early plantings) weeks prior to the last frost date. Your plants should be about 4 to 5 weeks old at the time of transplanting. Where I am currently living, the last frost date is April 20, so I start my plants the first week in March and transplant them to the garden the first week in April. I space them 18 inches apart in rows 24 inches apart.

¶ Prepare the soil by adding organic matter such as peat moss and an 8–10–8 fertilizer at the rate of 2 to 3 pounds in each 10-by-10-foot plot.

¶ Transplant the seedlings into Wallo'Waters (for extra-early plantings — 6 to 8 weeks prior to the last frost date) or cover with hotkaps (for usual plantings — 3 weeks prior to the last frost date). Since broccoli has large, spreading leaves, I remove the Wallo'Waters when the plants become crowded inside.

¶ Water the plants regularly. Broccoli has a somewhat shallow root system and will suffer severely if it does not receive adequate moisture. Establish a watering program that will never allow the soil to dry out, especially once the heads begin to develop.

¶ Harvest the broccoli when the heads have reached their maximum size but before the flowers have begun to open. If some flowers have opened, don't worry; they can still be eaten. Plan to harvest the broccoli about 11 to 12 weeks after starting your seed.

Pests and Disease

The two insects that most commonly bother broccoli are the flea beetles that attack radishes and the worm stage of a small white butterfly (cabbage looper) and various moths (cutworms). These pests chew holes in the leaves or feed on the head and generally reduce the health of the plant. Fortunately, all are easily controlled with rotenone (for beetles) and *Bacillus thuringiensis* in the form of Dipel, Thuricide, or BT (for worms). Other pests that occasionally attack broccoli are thrips, which cause the leaves to turn brownish and long-snouted weevils. (Weevils have never caused serious damage to my broccoli; they prefer the cabbage, especially the Chinese type.) When necessary, thrips can be controlled with insecticidal soap; and weevils with pyrethrum. On rare occasions during extended cool, moist periods, I have had limited problems with mildew and root rot.

Storing

Unlike many vegetables, broccoli cannot be stored fresh for long periods without a significant drop in quality, especially in taste. For best results, we rarely store broccoli in the refrigerator for more than 1 week, keeping it in a loosely closed plastic bag at 40° to 50°F. Be sure not to store broccoli in a paper sack, because the vegetable will rapidly lose water and wilt. Broccoli stored too long turns yellowish and smells and tastes strong.

Fortunately, broccoli is excellent for freezing and long-term storage. In fact, and contrary to some published advice, we have kept properly blanched broccoli for up to a year in the freezer and enjoyed it thoroughly. To prepare broccoli for long-term storage, wash and cut it into small portions, checking closely to remove any cabbage loopers that may be in the head. Don't let the kids see the loopers or worms at this stage or you may have trouble getting them to eat broccoli! Submerge the broccoli in boiling water for 3 minutes, place it in cold tap water (it doesn't have to be ice water) to cool, and then seal it in plastic bags. For our family of five, we usually put about 1 pound of broccoli in each bag. By preparing broccoli this way, you'll be enjoying it until next year's crop is ready.

Broccoli Varieties I Have Tested (my favorite,*)

Early Spartan	Good overall; produces nicely formed main head and nice crop of side heads
Green Comet*	Good overall; the well-formed heads are harvestable within 1 week; does not produce side heads to any degree
Green Duke	Good overall; heads are irregular and not as darkly colored as, say, the ones on Packman
Green Goliath*	Good overall; heads are nice size and well developed; harvestable over a period of 8 to 10 days; excellent crop of side heads
Packman*	Excellent overall; early producer of very uniform, flat-topped heads on short plants; heads mature at about the same time; excellent crop of side heads; my favorite for freezing; short, stocky, wind-resistant variety
Premium Crop*	Great overall; dense, dome-shaped heads; heads are harvestable at about the same time
Saga	Good overall; harvestable later than most

Others I have grown include Citation, Cruiser, and Waltham 29.

Brussels Sprouts

Although closely related to cabbage, brussels sprouts produces a small head at the base of each leaf; the heads have a slightly more robust flavor than cabbage. This vegetable is generally more tolerant of the cold than cabbage, often producing well into late fall and early winter in many areas. I recall picking sprouts in my garden in the Black Hills of South Dakota on Thanksgiving Day after several nights of 18° to 20°F temperatures.

Growing Essentials
The techniques for growing brussels sprouts are similar to those for broccoli with the following additions.

¶ Brussels sprouts must be grown so that most of the sprouts will

73

develop during cool weather. I put my plants out in the spring at the same time as broccoli and plan to harvest them in late May through mid-July. I then remove my plants completely since they do poorly in hot weather.

¶ For fall brussels sprouts, I start my plants about mid-June and transplant at the end of July. Protect transplants from the wind with boards, and be sure that they are not allowed to dry out.

¶ As sprouts develop, remove the leaves from the lower one-fourth of the plant. Never remove the upper leaves.

Pests and Diseases

The most serious pest of brussels sprouts is aphids. I spray my plants at least once a week with insecticidal soap to control them. Worms that attack brussels sprouts can be controlled with *Bt*.

Storing

Brussels sprouts can be blanched in boiling water for three minutes, cooled in water, and frozen. Sprouts may also be stored without blanching as radishes are; they will keep for several weeks.

Brussels Sprouts Varieties I Have Tested (my favorite,*)

Jade Cross Hybrid*	Excellent overall; produces abundant sprouts; very tolerant of the cold
Long Island Improved	Good production

Cabbage

The good news about growing cabbage is that many of the fungal and bacterial diseases (for example, blackleg and root knot) prevalent in other areas are less of a problem in the Great Plains, probably because the cool, wet conditions favorable to their development are uncommon. The bad news is that the period of cool weather in the spring when cabbage does best is usually shorter. This is not to say that cabbage is especially difficult to grow in the Heartland, because it isn't. We regularly enjoy wonderful dishes of steamed cabbage or cole slaw every spring and well into the summer since cabbage stores so well. Actually, the key to good cabbage production in a warm-weather area is simple: Start early. Cabbage also makes an excellent fall crop.

Growing Essentials

Follow the recommendations for broccoli (spring) or brussels sprouts (fall) along with this additional tip. Harvest when the heads have reached cantaloupe size or larger. If your heads begin to split, cut back on the watering.

Pests and Diseases

Cabbage is subject to attack by a broad variety of pests, including flea beetles (early on), long-snouted weevils, cutworms, and various leaf-eating worms (later on). Probably the most destructive of these pests are the cutworms, which will burrow into the head and do considerable damage before they are ever suspected. Cabbage loopers eat holes in the leaves. Fortunately, all of these pests are rather easily controlled with a combination of rotenone and pyrethrum for the weevils and *Bt* for the worms. For cutworms and loopers, be sure to apply *Bt* every week, regardless of whether you see worms; they will eventually arrive, and if you wait until you see them, the damage will be done. *Bt* will also kill other worms that damage cabbage leaves (for example, webworms).

Storing

One of the best features of cabbage is that it can be stored for long periods of time. We simply wash the heads thoroughly, wrap each head in plastic wrap, and store them in the refrigerator at 40° to 50°F. Heads stored this way should keep at least 2 to 3 months.

Cabbage Varieties I Have Tested
(my favorite,*; season — E, early; M, mid; or L, late)

Copenhagen Market[M]	Produces nice, solid heads
Emerald Cross*[,E]	Excellent overall; produces heavy, nicely formed heads; good flavor
Golden Acre*[,E]	Excellent overall; produces heavy, nicely formed heads; good flavor
Stonehead*[,L]	Excellent for fall gardens
Tastie*[,E]	Excellent overall; produces heavy, nicely formed heads that store extremely well; great flavor
Two Seasons Chinese*[,E]	Excellent overall (one head grew to 9 pounds!); be warned — every pest loves to eat it, especially long-snouted weevils

I have also grown Yellows Resistant Meteors.

Cauliflower

The exact origin of cauliflower is unknown, although research indicates that it developed from a form of broccoli somewhere in Europe during the Middle Ages. Gerard, in his 1633 herbal, mentioned "Cole flore, or after some Colieflore" and noted that "in the middest of which leaves

riseth vp a great white head of hard floures clossely thrust together."
Clearly, by the seventeenth century, gardeners were enjoying the
benefits of cauliflower. Interestingly, Gerard wrote that eating cauliflower would cure everything from bad eyesight and hearing to a
hangover!

Growing Essentials

I use essentially the same techniques for growing cauliflower as I do for
broccoli. Although I have frequently read that cauliflower is much more
difficult to grow than broccoli, I have not found this to be the case, at
least in my garden. It is true in my experience, however, that cauliflower
is less able to tolerate heat than broccoli.

¶ Start planting early. It is important that the cauliflower reaches
maturity before hot weather arrives, so timing is especially critical.

¶ As the heads begin to develop (about 1 inch), pull the outer leaves up
around them so direct sunlight will not reach the heads. This procedure
keeps the heads white, or blanches them. The leaves can be easily held
together by tying them with string or with rubber bands. If the heads are
not protected, they will turn yellowish or brownish; the additional heat
will probably also cause them to be bitter tasting. Self-blanching
varieties of cauliflower have wrapper leaves that curl over the head and
provide natural protection without tying.

¶ Cauliflower must be watered regularly, and once the heads begin to
develop it is especially important to never let the soil dry out. The heads
develop amazingly fast, and depriving the plant of sufficient water will
result in inferior heads.

¶ Harvest heads before they begin to break or turn off-color. Usually, a
head will go from 1 inch across to maturity in 12 to 16 days. Of course,
you can harvest them anytime in between if you wish.

Pests and Diseases

The pests and diseases that affect cauliflower are the same as those that
affect broccoli. Follow the same treatment.

Storing

Use the same methods you would for broccoli.

Cauliflower Varieties I Have Tested (my favorite,*)

Hybrid Snow King*	Produces great, tasty heads
Snow Crown Hybrid*	Harvestable earlier than most; excellent heads
Super Snowball	Heads smaller and harvestable later than Snow Crown

Violet Queen*	Sold as purple cauliflower but is actually a variety between cauliflower and broccoli; grows great, looks beautiful, and tastes like broccoli; heads don't need to be tied like standard cauliflower

I have also grown Extra-Early Snowball and Ravella.

Cantaloupe and Watermelons

The cantaloupe and closely related muskmelon are warm-season vegetables that belong to a single botanical species, *Cucumis melo*. Their fruits have a sweet, green- or orange-colored flesh at maturity that is unsurpassed in a fruit bowl. I can think of few more delicious treats at breakfast than a bowl of chilled cantaloupe slices and strawberries. Originally a native of Asia, the cantaloupe was introduced into North America by Columbus. There are many varieties of cantaloupe, including types developed specifically for home gardens and for shipping and marketing. Some have a smooth white rind, some yellow netted rinds, and still others dark-green wrinkled rinds. Although most market varieties probably average 2 to 4 pounds, some, such as Santa Claus, reach 8 to 10 pounds. Many varieties are now resistant to cantaloupe-destroying fungi such as downy and powdery mildews, rusts, and wilts.

The watermelon is a member of the melon family that requires longer periods of sustained warmth to develop than the cantaloupe, growing best where the soil is also quite warm. Apparently native to Africa, it was first introduced into North America in the early l600s. Although sometimes lumped together with cantaloupe, watermelons are only distantly related (species *Citrullus lanatus*); cantaloupe and cucumbers are more closely related to one another than to watermelons.

Growing Essentials

¶ Select a spot in a well-drained (use a raised bed if necessary), sunny location. Cantaloupe and watermelons require a rich soil for their best growth; they do especially well in sandy soils. Prepare your plot by adding lots of organic matter, such as compressed peat moss, until the soil is spongy. In a newly broken 10-by-10-foot plot, I would add at least 4 cubic feet of compressed peat, wheat straw, or cured, sterilized cow manure (if you know the source). Then add at least 4 pounds of a 5–10–5, 8–10–8 or equivalent fertilizer and mix it thoroughly into the soil.

¶ Dig a hole 5 inches deep, place $1/4$ cup of an 8–10–8 fertilizer in the bottom, and refill the hole with soil.

¶ Place 6 or 7 seeds in a hole 1 inch deep, cover with soil, and water thoroughly. After germination, each planting should be thinned to only 3 seedlings. Allow at least 4 feet between plantings. Compact-growing bush varieties of cantaloupe, watermelon, and other vine crops (for

77

example, cucumber) are now available, and you might want to try some of these varieties if your space is limited.

¶ Place hotkaps over the plantings. This will warm the soil and speed germination as well as protect the seedlings from wind when they emerge. Be sure to cut a small slit in the top of each hotkap at planting. The opening can be enlarged as the plants grow.

¶ For extra-early fruit, seeds can be planted outside in Wallo'Waters 2 or 3 weeks prior to the last-frost date. Put Wallo'Waters in place 10 to 12 days prior to planting to warm the soil.

¶ If desired, the plot can be covered with clear plastic and the seeds planted through slits in the plastic. The plastic will act as a mulch, conserving moisture in the soil and discouraging weed growth. The presence of the plastic has been shown by research studies to clearly speed up the growth of the plants and the first picking. The total fruit yield remains the same, however, with or without the plastic.

¶ Be sure that your plants receive plenty of moisture during the growing season. Since the fruits are composed mostly of water, their quality can be severely affected by drought.

¶ Cantaloupe and watermelon will run widely if allowed. After your vines have spread sufficiently (4 or 5 feet), trim the tips of the vines with a knife or scissors to encourage your vines to set fruits.

¶ I harvest my cantaloupe when I can smell a sweet aroma at the stem end. The fruit will often slip easily from the stem at this point. Ripe watermelons usually give a dull, hollow sound when they are thumped; if the melon is immature, the sound will be sharp. Another way to tell is by the color of the bottom. When immature the spot will be white or greenish white; as the melon ripens, the bottom gradually turns yellow or yellowish-orange.

Pests and Diseases

Spotted and striped cucumber beetles, squash bugs, and squash vine borers may attack your plants. I have found that a regular dusting (every 5 days) with rotenone and *Bt* at the base of the plants will control borers, and I eliminate cucumber beetles and squash bugs by handpicking them or spraying the plants with pyrethrum as needed. Other troublesome melon pests are mites and aphids, especially in hot weather. Control them by spraying the plants several times with an insecticidal soap. Most fungal diseases can be controlled by planting resistant varieties; if any fungal diseases appear, spraying with Bordeaux mixture is often effective against them.

Storing

Unfortunately, ripe cantaloupe and watermelon do not store well, and we usually do not keep them longer than 7 to 10 days. We found that they keep best when stored in a refrigerator at 40° to 50°F. Some varieties of cantaloupe can be picked green (netting should be fully developed) and allowed to ripen at room temperature. Leave about 2 inches of the stem attached and place the green melons in an open box in the light; the kitchen is fine. The fruits should ripen in 2 to 4 weeks.

Melon Varieties I Have Tested (my favorite,*; B, bush)

Cantaloupe

Harvest Queen*	Very productive but susceptible to mildews
Musketeer*,B	Very productive and sweet
Tam Uvalde*	Very productive and disease resistant; deep orange and sweet

I have also grown Burpee Super Hybrid.

Watermelon

Au-producer*	Excellent and disease resistant
Crimson Sweet*	Productive, great taste, and disease resistant; 10 to 21 pounds
Sugar Baby Small*	Icebox type; 6 to 10 pounds

Carrots It would be hard to imagine life without carrots. Eaten raw or in a wide variety of dishes including salads, meat entrees, and soups, carrots have a special flavor and texture unequaled by any other vegetable. They also contain high amounts of beta carotene, a substance some experts believe might help to prevent certain forms of cancer. Carrots are not planted as often by gardeners as their eating possibilities would suggest. This is probably due to the fact that carrots have a reputation — undeserved in my opinion — of being difficult to germinate, so many gardeners simply do not try. However, if they are given extra attention at planting, carrots are actually quite easy to grow.

Growing Essentials

¶ Before planting carrots, I add lots of organic matter and a combination of 8–10–8 and 0–20–0 fertilizers (about 1/2 cup of each for every 10-foot row) to the soil. The organic matter loosens the soil (especially important in clay soils) and allows the roots to penetrate easily. The high-phosphorus fertilizer encourages the development of strong, healthy roots.

¶ When planting your seeds, first dig a small trench 1/2 inch deep. After placing your seeds in the trench, cover them with 1/2 inch of good-quality potting soil, firming it gently. Water the soil and then cover

79

Did You Know?
Pollen

The Beautiful

Did you know that the reason some people are bothered by hay fever and the reason some gardeners have a problem getting their squash plants to set fruit are linked? The common factor is small packages called pollen, structures that protect and carry the genetic information from the male portion of the flower to the female. This movement of pollen from plant to plant is called pollination and may be accomplished by the wind or by insects. Some plants, such as corn, are pollinated primarily by the wind, whereas those with brightly colored flowers, such as cucumber, squash, okra, and eggplant, are generally pollinated by insects. If pollination does not happen, squash will not set fruit and corn will not fill out with plump kernels.

Pollen is remarkable stuff. Composed mainly of protein, pollen has several different layers that protect its internal contents from drying out. The internal contents of the pollen, including the male sperm cells, are necessary for fertilization and the development of seeds and fruits in most plants. The protein in pollen causes hay fever, as the immune system in your body reacts to foreign protein in the delicate linings of your nose and lungs.

The Practical

¶ If you are having trouble getting your squash plants to set fruit, you can cause pollination by hand. Locate a male flower (the one without a small green fruit below the flower) and remove the outside yellow petals; be sure to leave the inner, central column that holds the pollen. If you look closely at the column, you can see the pollen on the surface. Touch the column to the central area (the stigma) of a female flower (the one with a small green fruit below the flower), making sure some pollen stays behind on the stigma. Within 1 to 2 days, you should see a

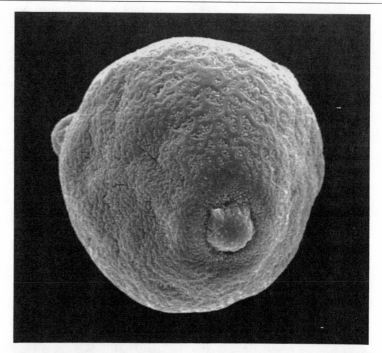

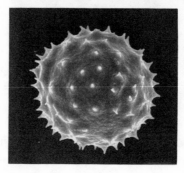

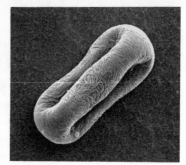

squash fruit begin to enlarge and develop.

¶ Tomatoes and eggplants can sometimes be encouraged to set more fruit by gently tapping the flowers so pollen is transferred from the male to the female parts of the flower.

¶ Be careful when using pesticides that kill bees (for example, Sevin and pyrethrum); you could prevent pollination.

¶ Plant extra flowers in your yard to encourage visits to your garden by insect pollinators such as bees (see appendix 2 for suggested flower varieties).

¶ Plant corn in blocks rather than long rows. This will encourage better pollination since more pollen will probably be blown from one plant to the next. Also, you might plant corn in the section of the garden that normally receives the most wind.

Aside from its importance in the development of seeds and fruits, pollen is beautifully varied. Pollen from okra (opposite, bottom left, magnified 700 times), dill (opposite, bottom right, magnified 1,200 times), bean (opposite top, magnified 2,000 times), geranium (above, magnified 1,800 times), phlox (lower left, magnified 1,050 times), and oregano (lower right, magnified 900 times) illustrate the intricacy and diversity of pollen grains.

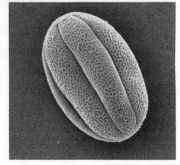

everything with a length of plastic wrap secured at the edges by boards. Planted this way, the seeds will remain moist and should germinate in 12 to 15 days. Remove the plastic wrap when seedlings appear. Space the rows about 12 inches apart.

¶ About 3 to 4 weeks after the carrots emerge, thin the plants so they stand about 1 inch apart. As with all root crops, thinning is very important if you want them to develop rapidly to a nice, uniform size. Eat the thinned baby carrots whole or use them in salads.

¶ Fertilize about every 2 weeks with a water-soluble fertilizer (for example, 15–30–15).

¶ If you use a carrot variety that elongates considerably, remember that in soils with a high-clay content, carrots may be difficult to remove at maturity. Use a shovel or fork when harvesting this type to prevent breakage of the roots.

Pests and Diseases

The two pests that attack carrots most commonly are grasshoppers, which eat the tops, and weevil larvae, which burrow into the roots. Both pests can be eliminated with a combination of rotenone and pyrethrum. Roots that have been damaged by burrowing larvae can still be used if the affected portions are trimmed.

Storing

Although carrots with their tops removed will keep for long periods in the refrigerator, I usually leave most of my carrot crop in the ground. After the first heavy frost in the fall, I cover my carrots with at least 6 inches of leaves, a layer of plastic, and boards to hold everything in place. Protected this way, the carrots and the ground around them will remain unfrozen even though air temperatures may drop well below 0°F. We usually dig our last carrots in late March, just in time to plant a new crop.

Carrot Varieties I Have Tested
(my favorite,*; length — L, long; M, medium; or S, short)

Danvers Half Long*,M	Productive and keeps well; good flavor
Gold Pak*,L	Grows well but elongates considerably and may be difficult to remove from tight soils; add plenty of organic matter to loosen soil
Nantes Coreless*,M	Nice and uniform and keeps well; good flavor
Royal Chanteny*,M	Good especially for clay soils; keeps well in the ground
Scarlet Nantes*,M	Productive

I have also grown Amsterdam Minicor[S], Chanteny Red Cored[M], Clarion[L], Lindora[L], and Sierra Hybrid[L].

Top: Children and vegetable gardens are a natural combination.
Bottom, left: A small beginning garden I had in Texas in 1972. Situated outside the kitchen window of our apartment, this garden was the perfect size to produce a regular supply of fresh vegetables for our table.

Bottom, right: Mid-season in my large Kansas garden in 1988. Located off the deck of our house, this spacious garden has plenty of room for a wide variety of vegetables that provide not only abundant fresh vegetables for the table but plenty for storage too.

Top, left: Early spring in my Great Plains garden. Tall, cone-shaped Wallo'Waters provide protection from wind and cold and an ideal, warm growing environment for young transplants of pepper, tomatoes, and head lettuce. Shorter hotkaps provide primarily wind protection for young, cold-hardy broccoli transplants.
Top, right: A soaker hose in action.

These hoses bleed water from their surface and are excellent devices for watering and deep soaking a Heartland garden with minimal loss due to evaporation. I would normally cover my soaker hoses with a mulch.
Bottom, left: Using trenches for deep-soaking Great Plains gardens is a good water conservation technique, especially when the trenches are covered

with a mulch. Note the bubbler that fits on the end of the hose and prevents soil erosion by the water stream.
Bottom, right: What a difference it makes when plants are protected! To the immediate left of the trowel is a lettuce plant grown in a hotkap; to its left are two plants grown without protection. The protected plant is fully twice the size of the unprotected plants.

Top, left: A flowering Early Girl tomato plant pushing itself out of a Wallo'Water the first week in May in Kansas. This plant was transplanted into the garden under the Wallo'Water in early April only one week after a March blizzard.
Top, right: In one of my small gardens in the foothills in Colorado, Wallo'Waters not only protected my transplants from the elements but also provided a conve-

nient drinking station for magpies.
Bottom, left: The wheat straw mulch in the right half of this squash patch not only conserves moisture but also acts as a barrier to weeds. The unmulched portion in the left half has a carpet of a pesky, nutrient- and water-robbing weed called prostrate spurge.
Bottom, right: In this photograph taken on a cold, snowy mid-March day are

Wallo'Waters in which I had planted young transplants of Ithaca head lettuce the day before. Much to the surprise of most visitors to my garden, by the first week in May I had beautiful heads of lettuce.

Left: One of my favorite garden friends, a praying mantis, eating a moth among a gorgeous array of composite flowers.

Above: Adult ladybugs, a garden friend everyone recognizes, among its less well-known black-and-orange-spotted larvae. The adults and larvae terrorize many garden pests, eating soft-bodied types like aphids and the larvae and eggs of others as well.

Top, left: Squash bugs damage vine crops by using their piercing-sucking mouth parts to extract sap from plant tissues and fruits. Here a cluster of young gray nymph forms are seen sunning themselves on a zucchini leaf. In the nymph stage, squash bugs are especially vulnerable to a pyrethrum-based spray.

Middle, left: There are few things more disgusting in the garden than finding a large green hornworm that has stripped a tomato leaf or damaged a tomato fruit. Handpick these pests or dust them with Bacillus thuringiensis.

Bottom, left: A Colorado potato beetle on potatoes. These pests and their brownish-orange larvae are easily controlled with a dusting of rotenone or Bacillus thuringiensis.

Right: One of the worst pests of corn, the corn earworm tunnels around inside the husk wreaking havoc with the cob. Corn earworms can be controlled by dusting the silk regularly with rotenone or Bacillus thuringiensis.

Top: The bacterial speck seen on this Surprise tomato is one of the many diseases that may attack tomatoes. Good garden sanitation and not bunching your tomato plants together are the first lines of defense against such diseases.

Right: The white coating on the older leaves of this summer squash plant (upper half of photograph) is caused by a fungal infection of powdery mildew. This disease can be controlled by spraying with a solution of sulfur or Bordeaux mix.

Top: Disaster sometimes happens in the garden. In June 1984 severe winds and golfball-sized hail leveled my garden. In this picture taken the next day, only the stalks of the tomato plants (cages in foreground) remain.

Left: By late August careful revitalization had restored my hail- and wind-damaged garden. Note the tomato plants in the foreground — recovered from the original plants — and corn toward the middle of the garden — replanted as seed.

Above, left: My son Scotty proudly showing off a head of Jung's Snow Crown Hybrid cauliflower grown in our garden in the middle of the Great Plains. If your timing is right you can grow any vegetable in the rich soils of this region.

Above, middle: Here I am harvesting a bumper crop of 3- to 4-pound Porto Rico sweet potatoes.

Above, right: Broccoli by the wheelbarrow — that's what Great Plains gardening can produce! The Packman variety shown here is especially well adapted to windy areas.

Right: My daughter Heather harvesting Early Girl and Jet Star tomatoes during a late September snowstorm in Kansas.

An early October harvest of vegetables from my Colorado foothills garden in 1989. From left: Big Bertha peppers, Scarlet Turnip White-tipped radishes, Better Boy tomatoes, Oregon Sugar Pod peas, Buttercrunch lettuce, and Early Prolific Straightneck squash.

The ideal tomato plant — lots of fruits and a minimum of foliage. Note that this Early Girl tomato is supported in a square cage.

Above: Sweet banana peppers — one of my favorites and a prolific producer in the Heartland.

Right: In one experiment to compare potato production, I planted whole small potatoes and the small sets or "chips" sold by many mail order companies. In this photograph each group of new potatoes (clockwise from top left: Norgold, Viking, Red Pontiac, Kennebec, Mayfair, and Norchip) was harvested from a single hill (note the penny in the center). Can you guess which groups came from original plantings of whole potatoes and which came from sets? As you might suspect, the large groups are from whole potatoes and the small groups are from sets. What a difference!

Overleaf: An award-winning harvest of vegetables from one of my Kansas gardens.

Celery, Dill, and Parsley

Although celery and parsley might seem out of place in the Great Plains, I can assure you that all three vegetables can be grown readily. Like the other members of the carrot family, these plants have highly dissected leaves with broad stalks and are very aromatic when crushed; consequently, they are often used as spices.

Growing Essentials

¶ Celery takes a long time to reach maturity and must be started especially early. In Kansas, I start my seeds at the end of January, a full 14 to 15 weeks before the last spring frost (April 20). Parsley also takes a long time to grow to transplant size and should be started at least 10 weeks prior to the last frost date. I always plant dill from seeds after the last frost date.

¶ Fertilize the seedlings every 10 days with water-soluble fertilizer. Because celery and parsley take so long to grow to transplanting size, I usually repot my plants at least once after they are about 7 weeks old to prevent salt damage from fertilizers.

¶ Soil preparation is especially critical with celery. I add plenty of organic matter and at least 1 pound of 8–10–8 fertilizer to each 10 feet of row. Parsley and dill are less demanding then celery and will grow almost anywhere the soil is somewhat rich.

¶ About 2 weeks before the last frost date, transplant celery and parsley to the garden. Celery should be spaced about 12 inches apart and parsley about 18 inches. Some sources indicate that parsley transplants poorly, but I have found the opposite to be true.

¶ When the celery and parsley plants are about 10 to 12 inches tall, side-dress them with a 27–3–3 fertilizer.

¶ Celery plants must not be allowed to dry out. Their root systems are very shallow, and they should be kept moist. I plant celery in a poorly drained part of my garden where the water stands after a heavy rainstorm. Celery plants deprived of water turn bitter. Parsley and dill should receive adequate moisture, but they are not as fussy as celery. Parsley is an especially tough plant; I've seen the same plant withstand over a season both 105° and 20°F days with little damage.

¶ When celery plants are about 12 to 16 inches tall, I pile straw around the base of the plants and cover the stalks. This prevents the sun from striking the stalks which causes them to taste bitter.

¶ Dill can become quite weedy if allowed to flower and fruit; however, it is quite easy to control with a hoe.

¶ Parsley is a biennial (a plant that lives for 2 years), thus it should be covered in the fall and uncovered in the spring, when it will resume growth and flower.

Pests and Diseases

The principal pest of celery is the carrot weevil whose grubs burrow into and destroy the stalk. Control them by dusting the plants with rotenone and/or spraying them with pyrethrum. Parsley and dill are often host plants for the worms of the beautiful black swallowtail butterfly, and I usually do not destroy all of the worms I see for this reason. The worms are easily controlled with pyrethrum spray and by handpicking (be careful — they stink!).

Storing

After harvesting, celery should be thoroughly washed and most of the roots should be removed. Cut most of the leaves from the top and store it in a sealed plastic container at 40° to 50°F. Celery should keep well for at least a month. Parsley and dill keep nicely with little effort if they are cut and stored in sealed plastic containers in a refrigerator, but since parsley is so tolerant of the cold, I always use it from the garden late into the winter. Parsley and dill can be air-dried by hanging the plants in a warm, well-ventilated area out of the sun. After they have dried, crumble the plants and store them in closed containers in a freezer to preserve maximum flavor.

Celery, Dill, and Parsley Varieties I Have Tested (my favorite,*)

Celery	
Burpee's Tendercrisp*	Does great, often producing 3- to 7-pound bunches
Dill	
Mammoth*	Extremely prolific
Parsley	
Dark Moss Curled*	Tolerant of drought and very productive

Corn I frequently take my botany classes to visit my gardens. I explain the many advantages of gardening to them, and I give them demonstrations. One demonstration I perform is to compare the taste of fresh corn from my garden with that of corn I purchased the same day at the local grocery store. The response is always the same: they simply cannot believe how delicious ("real" as one student described it) sweet corn tastes when eaten fresh from the garden.

Corn wasn't always considered such excellent table fare. Gerard, in his 1633 herbal, commented that "...we may easily judge, that it nourisheth but little, and is of hard and euill digestion, a more conuenient food for swine than for men." How times have changed! The appearance of many hybrid sweet corn varieties undoubtedly influ-

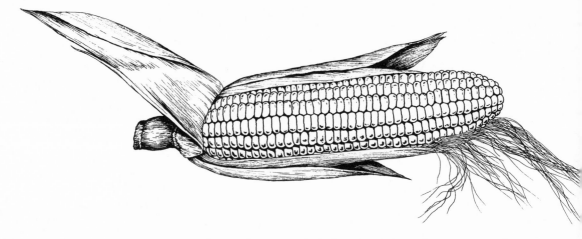

enced this change, but I can't help but think that a few seventeenth century gardeners must have appreciated better than others the true culinary delights of corn.

Although sweet corn can be grown in nearly all regions of the United States, it does particularly well in the warm areas of the Heartland, where it will grow in almost any soil that is rich and well drained enough to meet its needs. Even in marginal areas and soils, newer and more-productive hybrids often produce suitable crops, especially if the planting is timed correctly and if sufficient levels of nutrients are maintained.

Growing Essentials

¶ For best results, the soil should be warm and all danger of frost should be past when the seed is planted. When I gardened in the northern Black Hills of South Dakota, this was about the first or second week in June, whereas in west-central Kansas, it is about the first or second week of May. I have to tell you, however, that I often take a chance and cheat on this advice, planting corn in Kansas during the middle of April. If I am lucky, we eat fresh sweet corn the first week in July; if not, I lose a little seed and replant. I have also planted sweet corn in Kansas as late as the last week in June, and harvested great late-August to early-September roasting ears. When planting this late, it is especially important to select a variety that is tolerant of intense summer heat (for example, Jubilee).

¶ I fertilize my soil with 2 pounds each of 8–10–8 and 8–22–6 fertilizers in a 10-by-10-foot area. This combination seems to give the corn optimum levels of nitrogen for leaf and stem growth, of phosphorus for cob production, and of potassium for root growth.

¶ Corn should be planted in the full sun since it belongs to a group of plants (C_4 or Kranz) whose photosynthetic mechanisms work most efficiently under warm, bright conditions.

¶ In my experience, extra-early and early varieties of corn simply do not have the flavor that the midseason and later types have. Also, if you plant your corn in late June, be sure not to use one of the early varieties; they do not do well under hot, midsummer conditions.

¶ I have planted corn in hills (2 plants each after thinning), in groups in rows (2 plants each, 18 inches apart, after thinning), and in rows with individual plants thinned from 12 (early types) to 18 (later types) inches. I can honestly say that I have had good luck with each method and suggest that you try the method that appeals most to you. Always separate the rows or hills by 24 inches. It is essential that whatever method you use, you should thin the plants. Unthinned corn simply will not produce a good crop.

¶ Expect that at least once each summer your corn will be blown over during thunderstorms. Don't worry. Within a few days, the stalks will right themselves.

¶ Although I prefer the distinct corn taste of the standard varieties, you might try some of the sweeter types, which have genetic traits that increase the tenderness and sugar content of the kernals and slow the change of the sugars into starch. The genes are referred to as sugary enhanced (se), or Everlasting Heritage (EH), and shrunken (sh_2) genes. These varieties do not need to be isolated from normal corn when they're planted, but for maximum quality, sh_2 varieties should not be planted near other varieties. The sh_2 types are often referred to as supersweet corn, and, let me warn you, the sweeter varieties are sweet!

Pests and Diseases

Watch for pests and diseases from the time of planting until the time of harvest. Corn maggots will destroy seeds, but they can usually be thwarted by using treated seed. At later stages, the most serious pests are various worms that will attack the emerging seedlings (cutworms), stalks (corn borers), and ears (earworms). Although these are difficult to eradicate without resorting to synthetic pesticides, prudent use of *Bacillus thuringiensis*, rotenone, and pyrethrum controls them nicely. Corn earworm can be especially troublesome, and I have found that early-maturing varieties seem more susceptible than varieties that mature later in the season. To minimize corn earworm damage, begin dusting the silks with *Bt* or rotenone as soon as the silks appear and then once each week until harvest. The two most serious corn diseases in my experience are smut and stalk rot, both of which are caused by fungi. These are especially prevalent during wet periods and can be partially controlled by using raised beds and good sanitation. If you see smut on your corn, destroy the affected plants immediately, because the spores can survive for several years in the soil. The stalk rots are best controlled by planting resistant varieties.

Storing

There is simply no substitute for eating corn shortly after it has been harvested; our favorite way is to cook it in a pot of water that is boiling as I pick and clean the ears. However, we also enjoy the taste of sweet corn long after harvest, and this means long-term storage. We have had excellent luck with long-term storage of corn after it has been blanched. If the kernels have been removed from the cob, we boil them for 3 minutes before cooling and freezing them. But if we store the entire cobs, we first boil them for 12 to 14 minutes, then cool them in ice water for at least 10 minutes before freezing them. Corn prepared this way will keep for at least 4 to 6 months.

Corn Varieties I Have Tested
(my favorite,*; season — E, early; M, mid; or L, late)

Double Delicious*,M	An se type; productive and has great flavor; germinates weakly so plant it extra thick, preferably after the soil has been thoroughly warmed
Jubilee*,M	Produces large, well-filled ears with excellent flavor
Silver Queen*,L	Very productive with good flavor

I have also grown Earliking[E], Earlivee[E], Golden Cross Bantam[L], NK 199[L], Spirit Hybrid[E], Sterling Silver[L], and Sunglow[E].

Cucumbers Like many vegetables, the cucumber is not native to the United States. In fact, it is not even from the Western Hemisphere, having come instead from India. The exact history of the cucumber is obscure, but it was apparently introduced first into Europe well before the Middle Ages, and subsequently into the Americas. Although the nutritive value of the cucumber is somewhat limited since it is composed primarily of water, this vegetable is rich in vitamin C. Cucumber leaves have recently been shown to contain cholesterol reductase, an enzyme that breaks down cholesterol, but the significance of this discovery to human nutrition is uncertain. In addition to its excellent taste, the ease with which the cucumber is grown and its high productivity undoubtedly contribute to its popularity in the home garden.

Growing Essentials

During the seventeenth century, Gerard noted that growing a good crop of cucumbers required a bed of "hot and new horse dung," protection from "iniurie of the cold frostie nights," water that has "stood in the house or in the Sun a day before," because water "newly taken forth of a well or pumpe, will so chill and coole them" and, finally, a place in the garden "where the sun hath most force." Although we may be tempted to think that gardening has changed a great deal since Gerard's time, the needs of cucumbers as outlined by him have actually changed little if any. Rather, what we now enjoy are the increased benefits (for example, yield) of hybrids and disease-resistant varieties. If you observe the following instructions, I am certain you will harvest an abundance of cukes.

¶ Select your varieties carefully. Some cucumbers are very susceptible to fungal diseases and should be avoided since these diseases reduce

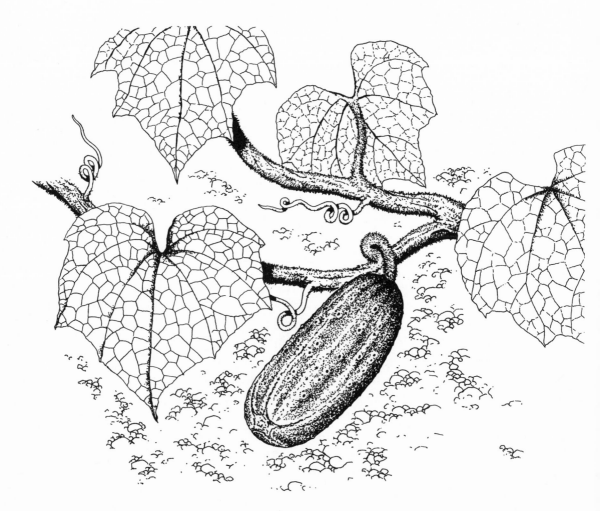

production in plants and significantly shorten the length of the growing season for affected plants.

¶ Prepare the soil by adding abundant organic matter such as peat moss or straw. Add 4 pounds of an 8–22–6 or equivalent fertilizer and mix it thoroughly in the upper 6 inches of each 10-by-10-foot area.

¶ Dig a hole 5 inches deep where the cucumbers will be planted, place ¼ cup of 8–22–6 or an equivalent fertilizer in the bottom of the hole, and refill it with soil.

¶ Place 4 to 5 seeds in a hole 1 inch deep and cover them with soil. Allow at least 3 to 4 feet between plantings. Although there is no effective control for the damping off of seedlings, selecting a planting site with adequate drainage will help.

¶ Cover each planting with a Wallo'Water or hotkap to protect the emerging plants from wind. For extra-early cucumbers, plant seeds in Wallo'Waters 2 weeks prior to the last frost date in your area. Plants should appear within 6 to 8 days if the ground is warm, but if you plant early and don't use a Wallo'Water or hotkap, it may take as long as 3 weeks. Leave the hotkaps in place and allow the plants to grow through the top. Wallo'Waters may be removed when the plants poke through the top, but wait as long as possible after the last frost date in your area.

¶ As your vines reach 4 to 5 feet in length, cut the growing ends off of the rapidly elongating stems. This will make your plants run less and produce fruit sooner.

¶ If desired, erect a trellis for the plants to climb. I use a large opening chicken wire formed in a semicircle for easy access. The trellis must be flexible but supported with metal, wood, or bamboo poles driven into the ground to prevent wind damage.

¶ Fertilize the plants every 2 weeks with a water-soluble fertilizer (for example, 15–30–15).

¶ Be sure to harvest all the fruits from your plants before they become overmature (they will have a yellowish or whitish cast). Leaving fruits past maturity will signal the plant that the end of the season is near, and the plant will stop producing fruits.

Pests and Diseases

Cucumber beetles are the most serious pest in my experience, although squash bugs can sometimes be a problem. Both can be effectively controlled with a combination of rotenone and pyrethrum. Cucumber beetles are especially troublesome because they are carriers (even during the winter) of bacterial wilt. Cucumbers affected by wilt show poor production and eventually die (some fungal diseases show similar symptoms). These beetles also spread mosaic viruses among cucumbers, causing stunted vines and mottled fruits. Usually late in the season, powdery mildew will attack your cucumber leaves and fruits (even resistant varieties), and other diseases, such as anthracnose and leaf spot (bacterial and fungal), may strike them at anytime. I have found that Bordeaux mixture is effective in controlling all of these diseases. Follow all directions carefully when using this compound.

Storing

Cucumbers are so productive that storage is rarely a problem. They do not store fresh for long periods of time, but will keep for 7 to 10 days in the refrigerator at 40° to 50°F. Cucumbers used for pickling should be no more than 24 hours old.

Cucumber Varieties I Have Tested (my favorite,*; P, pickler; S, slicer)

Bush Champion*,S	Good disease resistance; productive bush type
County Fair*,P	Excellent disease resistance; also resistant to cucumber beetles; productive, very mild, and "burpless"
Gemini*,S	Excellent disease resistance; very productive
Pioneer F1*,P	Excellent disease resistance; vigorous and highly productive
Poinsett*,S	Excellent disease resistance; great tasting fruits; highly productive
Sweet Slicer*,S	Good disease resistance

I have also grown Burpee Hybrid II^S, Liberty^P, Long Improved^S, Marketer^S, Marketmore 76^S, and Straight Eight^S.

Eggplants In one of my very first gardens many years ago in El Paso, Texas, plants often struggled because of the intense sun and heat. Yet, while some plants struggled to simply survive, others, such as eggplants and sunflowers, thrived. Eggplants are closely related to peppers and tomatoes and, like their cousins, they thrive in hot weather regions. If you are fortunate enough to live in an area of the Great Plains that has long, hot summers, you should have no trouble growing plenty of eggplants. In fact, you'll undoubtedly end up giving away more than you can ever use, thereby impressing everyone with your gardening abilities. You don't need to put out very many plants unless you have a market for the extras. One plant will often produce at least 20 ½-pound fruits over the course of a season. In our Kansas garden, my daughter, Heather, planted an eggplant in mid-May that produced the first harvestable fruit on July 30 and the last on November 9. In total, it produced 36 fruits!

Growing Essentials

¶ I start my eggplants at least 7 to 8 weeks before I plan to transplant them to the garden. In Kansas, this means that I start them the third week of March since I transplant them to the garden the second week of May.

¶ I've grown eggplants in every section of my garden with no special preparation other than mixing an 8–10–8 fertilizer into the soil at a rate of about 1 pound in each 4-by-4-foot area. The most important thing to remember is to place your plants where they will receive maximum sunlight and heat.

¶ Unless I use Wallo'Waters, I don't plant my eggplants until I am certain that the cold weather has passed and the soil is warm, about 2 to 3 weeks after the last frost date. Even then I cover my plants with hotkaps just in case. When using Wallo'Waters, I transplant eggplants about 3 weeks prior to the last-frost date. Eggplants will be quite large and spreading, so provide at least 5 to 8 square feet of space for each plant.

¶ Although eggplants are very resistant to drought, don't forget to water them. I deep soak them at least once a week, since their large leaves and fruit production produce a considerable water drain on these plants. Plants may survive if you fail to water them, but don't expect good fruit production.

¶ You can harvest eggplants when the skins are purplish-black and shiny. A dull skin usually indicates that the fruit is overripe and seedy. Don't allow mature fruits to remain on the plant since this will slow production.

Pests and Diseases

Grasshoppers, cucumber beetles, flea beetles, and mites are the biggest problems to eggplants in warm-weather areas. I use rotenone or pyrethrum-based sprays to deal with grasshoppers and beetles, and insecticidal soaps for mites. Be certain that you look for the presence of mites early (as soon as hot weather arrives) since they are easier to treat when the infestation is not too severe. Occasionally, my plants have been affected by anthracnose and blight.

Storing

Unfortunately, eggplants do not store well. Be careful not to handle them roughly, as undamaged eggplants keep best. We usually keep them in the lower part of the refrigerator and use them as quickly as possible.

Did You Know?

Insects and Pollination

The Beautiful

The yellow, powdery pollen that most flowers produce is extremely important for developing the fruits of many vegetables in the garden (see Did You Know? Pollen, p. 80). Although the transfer of pollen, or pollination, in plants such as corn is done primarily by the wind, plants such as squash depend almost entirely on insects (bees and so on) to move their pollen from plant to plant. For this reason, the importance of protecting these beneficial insects in your garden cannot be underestimated. How is pollen moved on insects? If you examine a bee closely, you can see that its surface is quite hairy, a natural trap for small structures like pollen, especially if the surface of the pollen is rough or sticky (for example, in squash and okra). The features of both the bee and the pollen insure that a bee visiting a flower will carry pollen to the next flower it visits and thereby cause fruit to set.

The Practical

¶ Try to avoid the use of insecticides that kill beneficial insects such as bees, or, if some must be used (for example, pyrethrum), use during the late evening when bees are less active.

¶ Encourage insects such as bees to visit your garden by planting small flower gardens (see appendix 2 for suggested flower varieties) within or around it. You might even install a small hive in your yard if the situation is acceptable (that is, no small children to be stung or neighbors who object) and if local ordinances allow beekeeping in residential areas.

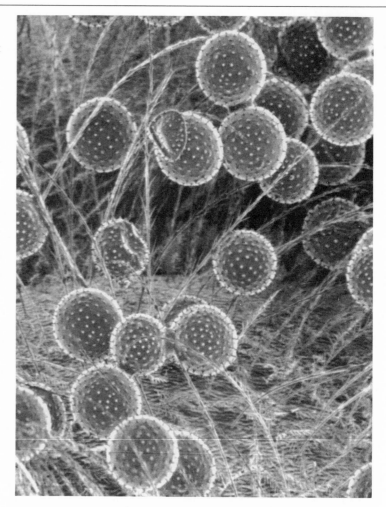

This honey bee (head, right, magnified 32 times) was captured immediately after visiting a zucchini flower. Abundant pollen can be seen attached to hairs on the bee's back (above, magnified 102 times). This should help you appreciate the value of bees in carrying pollen throughout the garden and may demonstrate why pesticides that kill bees should not be used carelessly.

Eggplant Varieties I Have Tested (my favorite,*)

Black Beauty*	Great overall; produces abundant 1- to 1½-pound fruits over a long season; excellent flavor; vigorous
Midnite	Good overall but starts slowly
Satin Beauty	Good overall; produces nice 1- to 1½-pound fruits

Huckleberries Sometimes called blackberries or swartzberries in the Great Plains, the berries of this plant are prized in many ethnic (especially German-Russian) recipes. Known in scientific circles as *Solanum nigrum,* the huckleberry is related to the potato and grows wild throughout much of North America. It is still reported in some books as being a poisonous plant, but based on the large number of people who have eaten the ripe berries with no ill effects, this "poisonous" label is hardly appropriate.

Growing Essentials

¶ Huckleberries can become a serious weed in the garden, so try to grow them in a spot where their fruits will not spread easily.

¶ Although they will grow in practically any soil, I always grow mine in a loamy soil to which I have added 4 pounds of 8–10–8 or an equivalent fertilizer for each 10-by-10-foot area. Plant several seeds in holes about 18 inches apart in a sunny part of the garden.

¶ The plants are quite tolerant of drought but do benefit from regular watering, especially after fruits begin to develop.

¶ Berries can be harvested after they turn bluish-black. Do not use the green berries, because they can cause digestive upset. Be sure to save a few ripe fruits with seeds for planting in next year's garden.

Pests and Diseases

Flea beetles will rapidly destroy young seedlings, but once the plants are established, little seems to bother huckleberries. Flea beetles are readily controlled with rotenone. Birds enjoy ripe huckleberries, and you may have to cover them with netting if they cause serious damage.

Storing

Huckleberries can be washed and frozen or stored fresh for short periods of time. I like to use mine fresh.

Huckleberry Varieties I Have Tested

Huckleberry seeds can be purchased from mail-order houses, but I originally received my seeds from my mother-in-law. I suspect they are merely the wild species that grows in our area.

Leafy Greens: Lettuce, Spinach, and Swiss Chard
Although not all botanically related, lettuce (leaf and head), spinach, and Swiss chard share a feature: We grow and eat them for their leaves. These leafy vegetables are delicious alone or combined with other vegetables in salads; with the exception of head lettuce, they are also easy to grow and can tolerate abuses of weather, such as hail, that decimate other vegetables. Once harvested, all three varieties will keep for weeks in the refrigerator with little effort.

The almost sweet to mild flavor of lettuce is hard to describe, but it easily complements the flavor of almost any other food. It is an extremely popular vegetable, and even in the Heartland, where the extremes of weather are severe, it is rarely absent in the home garden. The flavor of spinach and Swiss chard are more robust than lettuce, which probably explains why they are not grown as frequently.

Growing Essentials for Leaf Lettuce, Spinach, and Swiss Chard

¶ Lettuce and spinach are cool-weather plants that are very tolerant of the cold. Therefore, plan to plant some of each as early as 4 to 8 weeks before the last frost date, and continue to plant some every 2 weeks until the last frost date or shortly thereafter. Unlike the first two, Swiss chard

95

grows well under both cool and warm conditions and is especially tolerant of hot weather. It may be planted from early spring through late summer.

¶ Prepare your soil by thoroughly mixing in plenty of organic matter (for example, 2 cubic feet of compressed peat) and 3 pounds of 27–3–3 fertilizer to each 10-by-10-foot area. Swiss chard does well in limy soils.

¶ Plant your seeds in a trench about $1/4$ inch deep and cover them with soil. Allow 12 inches between rows. Firm the soil lightly over the seeds and water thoroughly by sprinkling. In the early spring, cover only with a plastic wrap and secure the edges from the wind; this warms the soil and speeds germination. If you cover it in this way in the summer, it will heat the soil to the point that germination is prevented. Regardless of the planting date, be sure the soil stays moist until the seeds germinate; water under the plastic if necessary.

¶ When the seedlings begin to emerge, remove the plastic wrap. Water with a water-soluble fertilizer (for example, 15–30–15) every 10 days.

¶ About 2 to 3 weeks after the plants emerge, thin the leaf lettuce to 4 inches, the spinach to 2 inches, and the chard to 10 inches. Some people do not thin any of these (or other vegetables, for that matter), but try it once, and you'll see that your plants will be much more productive. I always tell gardeners that raising plants in a garden is like raising farm animals. If you tried to raise 500 chickens in a pen, where they were standing side by side, you would probably end up with a bunch of scrawny, sickly fryers when they reached maturity. The same is true with plants. Give them adequate room (by thinning) to grow without having to compete with each other for light, nutrients, and water, and they'll be healthy and productive.

¶ Harvest any of these vegetables once the leaves are large enough to use. If you keep your plants well watered, you'll be able to harvest lettuce and spinach until the weather gets warm and your plants bolt (produce flower stalks); chard will grow throughout the season without bolting.

Pests and Diseases

Damage to leaf lettuce, spinach, and Swiss chard in my gardens has usually been the result of slugs (in cooler regions like South Dakota), worms, and tip burn.

Storing

Leaf lettuce, spinach, and Swiss chard will keep for up to 4 to 6 weeks if they are washed, drained of excess water, and placed in a closed plastic container in a refrigerator at 40° to 50°F. Check periodically and remove any leaves that show signs of decay.

Growing Essentials for Head Lettuce

I am convinced that anyone can grow beautiful head lettuce, even in areas of the Heartland where the temperature and the wind frequently conspire to prevent the growth of any plant. Just remember that lettuce, like any other vegetable, requires certain conditions for optimal growth. I have found these steps successful in growing head lettuce.

¶ Prepare the soil by mixing in generous amounts of organic matter and fertilizer prior to planting. To each 10-by-10-foot area, I add 4 cubic feet of compressed peat moss and 3 pounds of an 8–10–8 or equivalent granular fertilizer.

¶ Start your seeds indoors about 4 weeks prior to planting and about 7 weeks prior to the last frost date.

¶ Be sure the starting mix you use has been sterilized or has a fungicide to prevent damping-off, a disease that lettuce seedlings seem particularly susceptible to.

¶ Transplant to the garden 3 weeks prior to the last frost date, allowing 12 inches between plants and rows. Use hotkaps! If desired, you can transplant into Wallo'Waters even earlier (8 weeks). I cannot overemphasize the importance of planting early and using protection against wind for successfully and consistently growing great head lettuce.

¶ Water regularly. Head lettuce needs a continual supply of moisture to do well and to form solid, crisp heads. I occasionally fertilize with a water-soluble fertilizer (for example, 15–30–15).

¶ Harvest and chill your lettuce; then invite the neighbors and relatives over for a taste test. I hand each person a slip of paper and pieces of several different lettuces (numbered only) and ask them to evaluate the variety for taste and texture. I find that this is the surest way to get an honest opinion on a particular variety. Results are amazingly consistent, as, for example, in the case of Ithaca lettuce. Eighty percent of the people I had taste this lettuce rated it as sweet, with the remaining 20 percent ranging from mild to sweet. No one ever said it had a strong or bitter taste. Little wonder it is my favorite lettuce.

Pests and Diseases

Occasionally I have a problem with slugs or cutworms in lettuce heads, but treating the plants with *Bt* generally solves it. Pill bugs (roly-polies) also cause minor damage to outside leaves and sometimes get into the heads. Although they are unsightly, they have never been a serious enough problem to require the application of a pesticide. Fungal diseases have never been a problem, and only rarely have I had to remove and discard a plant due to tipburn.

Storing

Although lettuce will dry out and deteriorate rapidly if it isn't refrigerated, it will keep for weeks under the proper conditions. I rinse head, butterhead, and romaine lettuce, drain them thoroughly, and store them in the refrigerator at about 45°F in plastic bags in which I have punched several small holes. Stored in this manner, most lettuce will keep for a minimum of 2 to 4 weeks. As an alternative, I will occasionally separate the leaves in a head and store them in a sealed plastic container. The lettuce keeps about the same length of time but is handier to use, especially for the kids, who love to fix peanut butter and lettuce sandwiches — they're delicious!

Lettuce, Spinach, and Swiss Chard Varieties I Have Tested
(my favorite,*; CH, crisp head; BH, butterhead; L, leaf; or R, romaine)

Lettuce

Buttercrunch*,BH	An excellent, mild lettuce that does well under almost any conditions; this variety is a great compromise between head and leaf lettuce
Continuity CH	A robust-tasting lettuce with a beautiful burgundy color; would make an attractive ornamental
Grand Rapids*,L	A great, tasty lettuce that withstands the heat well; very productive
Great Lakes*,CH	A mild, tasty lettuce that produces solid, crisp heads about 1 to 1½ pounds each
Ithaca*,CH	A marvelous, easy-to-grow variety that produces solid, sweet heads about 1 to 1½ pounds each; has a crisp texture and is very resistant to disease and weather extremes; my favorite variety by far
New York 515*,CH	A mild lettuce that produces solid, crisp heads about 1 to 1½ pounds each; somewhat susceptible to tip burn
Parris Island*,R	A somewhat strong-tasting but nevertheless excellent cos or romaine lettuce; grows vigorously and produces solid 2-to-3-pound heads; very disease and pest resistant
Rosa*,CH	Very good taste and growth; matures later than most

I have also grown Crispino CH, Early Great Lakes CH, Iceberg CH, Imperial 44 CH, Montello CH, Ruby L, and Vanguard CH.

Spinach

Bloomsdale Long-Standing*	A good standard, productive type

Gurney's Hybrid No. 7	Does poorly in hot weather; bolts quickly
Tyee Hybrid*	A productive, excellent variety for hot-weather regions; does not bolt easily

Swiss Chard

Fordhook Giant*	Extremely productive and resistant to drought and heat; when the weather is so hot that nothing will grow, this will look great; also very tolerant of frosts

Okra   If you have a hot place in your garden, okra is the vegetable to plant there. Intolerant of cold and frosts, this heat-loving relative of the hollyhock and the red hibiscus will not even set fruit if the nights are cool. It is comparatively easy to grow and is so vigorous in most areas of the Great Plains that once it reaches maturity, its pods must be harvested daily to maintain their quality.

There are many varieties, including ones that are tall (up to 7 feet) or short, ones with short or long pods, and ones with variously colored pods. The names given to these cultivars are colorful themselves and include Emerald, Louisiana Green Velvet, and Annie Oakley.

The foliage of okra is attractive and, although short-lived, the flowers are large and quite beautiful. If you do not like yellow-jacket wasps, you should be forewarned that the foliage of okra exudes sticky substances that attract these insects. However, I consider these wasps a benefit since they are very effective predators of many leaf-eating worms.

Growing Essentials
¶ Select an area that receives a maximum amount of sunlight. An area next to a south-facing wall or fence that receives 8 or more hours each day is ideal.

¶ Okra will grow well in almost any well-drained, fertile soil. I always work plenty of organic matter and a combination of 1½ pounds each of 8–10–8 and 0–20–0 fertilizers into each 10-by-10-foot area prior to planting. If the clay content of the soil is high, adding sand and organic matter will improve the texture.

¶ Before planting, I soak my seeds overnight in tap water to soften the seed coat for improved germination.

¶ Be certain that the soil is warm before the seeds are planted. Okra simply will not grow well if the soil or the air are consistently cool. I learned from a gardening friend that by waiting until the soil and air temperatures were thoroughly warm, I could harvest bumper crops at the same time as when I planted earlier when everything was cooler.

¶ Plant your seeds in groups of 5 at least 18 inches apart in rows 24

99

inches apart. When the seedlings have at least 2 or 3 leaves, thin to 1 plant at each location.

Pests and Diseases

Pests love to bother okra. These include aphids, cutworms, flea beetles, corn earworms, cucumber beetles, and many others. As soon as the seedlings emerge, I apply a dusting of rotenone every few days until they are well established; I then apply pyrethrum (for chewing insects) or insecticidal soap (for aphids) as needed. Okra is very susceptible to damping-off in the seedling stage, and waiting until the soil is thoroughly warm helps prevent this problem.

Storing

Okra is best when used fresh (it is great mixed with eggs and then rolled in corn meal or flour and fried), but it will keep for 5 to 7 days if it is stored in a closed plastic bag in a refrigerator at 40° to 50°F. We store our excess by blanching the pods in boiling water for 4 minutes and then freezing them. A favorite way to preserve okra is to pickle it in a brine solution, but this is not recommended if you are on a low salt diet!

Okra Varieties I Have Tested (my favorite,*)

Annie Oakley*	Early and very productive; my first choice
Clemson Spineless*	Great producer of tender pods; a standard variety

I have also grown Cajun Queen.

The Onion Family: Onions, Chives, Garlic, and Shallots

Members of the onion family all have bulbs (an underground stem that produces fleshy leaves) that often have pungent odors and flavors. Used primarily in historical times to obscure the taste and smell of rotten meat, they are now prized additions to many culinary dishes from stews to pizzas. Onions, chives, garlic, and shallots are cool-season vegetables, and so must do a considerable part of their early growth of tops during cool weather. Healthy tops will insure the highest quality in bulbs that develop primarily during warm weather.

Generally, onions are classified as bunching, multiplying, storage, or sweet. Bunching onions (also called scallions or green onions) are usually planted from seed and never form a large bulb. These can be harvested over several years. Multiplier onions include varieties that, as the name implies, produce a cluster of small to large bulbs that cling together — you literally plant one and harvest many. Garlic and shallots are members of this group. Shallots resemble garlic, but the former have a more delicate flavor and can be used like onions. Garlic and shallots are good keepers. Storage onions — yellow, white, or purple — characteristically form a large bulb that will keep for several months; the yellow are generally the best for winter storage. Sweet onions also produce large bulbs, but they have low levels of sulfur (this causes the pungent odor and taste of onions) and as a result are sweet. Sweet varieties include Walla Walla and Vidalia. These onions are not good keepers. Both storage and sweet onions can be harvested early and used as green onions. Finally, chives, a perennial member of the onion family, produces clusters of beautiful purple flowers and makes a colorful addition to the vegetable garden.

Growing Essentials

¶ Select a sunny, well-drained spot and add plenty of organic matter and an 8–10–8 or similar fertilizer at the rate of 2 pounds in each 10-by-10-foot plot.

¶ Plant the sets, cloves, or plants (onions should be spaced closely; garlic and shallots 4 to 5 inches apart) as soon as the soil can be worked, usually at least 6 to 8 weeks before the last frost date. Allow 12 inches between rows, and thin the onions later to 4 to 5 inches within rows. Although late frosts and freezes may damage leaves, don't worry: these vegetables will recover. It's better to be too early rather than too late in planting onions and their kin.

¶ Provide the plants with plenty of moisture throughout their development. If onions taste too hot, it is probably because they weren't watered enough during growth. Occasionally fertilize the plants with a water-soluble fertilizer (for example, Miracle-Gro).

¶ Harvest the bulbs of onions, garlic, and shallots for storage when the tops have yellowed or whitened and fallen over. Leave them in the open, out of the sun, until the tops are completely dry, and then place the bulbs in a warm, well-ventilated area to cure for 7 to 10 days. Onion bulbs that are stored before the tops are completely dry and cured may develop a disease known as neck rot.

¶ Chives are harvested by clipping the pungent tops to use in salads or in toppings on other vegetables. Chives are easily dug up, divided, and planted at various places in the garden or shared with friends.

Pests and Diseases

Onion thrips and maggots may damage these vegetables during growth. Thrips, which are most common in warmer areas, can be eliminated by spraying the plant tops with pyrethrum. The worst problems I had with onion maggots were in the cooler areas of the Heartland (for example,

101

Did You Know?
Stinging Insects

The Beautiful
Most gardeners have been bothered by stinging or biting insects if they have gardened for very long. Mostly, it has been by pesky mosquitoes, but occasionally some of us have had the misfortune of encountering the stinging end of a bee or wasp. Although the sting was painful, it might interest you that you just experienced in the stinger one of those absolutely marvelous structures found in nature.

The Practical
¶ If you don't disturb stinging insects such as bees and wasps, they won't sting you. Both are beneficial in the garden — bees help to set fruit and wasps attack and destroy harmful worms.

¶ If you are stung by a bee, remember that the stinger will remain embedded in your flesh, so it should be removed to prevent further irritation.

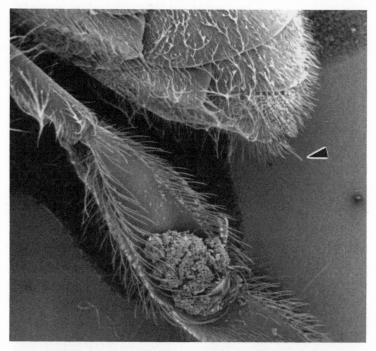

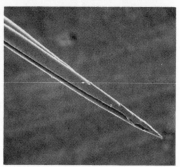

Every gardener knows that a bee's stinger is at the back end of the insect (upper, magnified 25 times). Looking closely at a bee's stinger (lower left, magnified 225 times) one can see backward-pointing barbs, much like those on a fishhook, which insure that the stinger will not be easily removed. On the other hand, a wasp's stinger is smooth (lower right, magnified 100 times). Isn't it amazing that something that causes such pain can be so remarkably beautiful?

Colorado and South Dakota). To help prevent them, I dusted my bulbs at planting and then weekly with rotenone and *Bt*.

Storing

These bulb vegetables should be stored in a cool, dry, well-ventilated location. They store for different lengths of time — sweet or bermuda onions for 1 to 2 months; thick-skinned, long-storage types for 5 to 8 months; and garlic and shallots for 8 months or longer. We keep ours in collapsible, plastic-coated, wire baskets available at many discount stores.

Onion, Chive, Garlic, and Shallot Varieties I Have Tested

I must admit that I have always grown onions, garlic, and shallots from sets available at local grocery and discount stores in the spring. These are usually the Stuttgarter or Ebenezer (yellow, long-term storage) or Eclipse (green onions and white, short-term storage) varieties. The garlic I plant comes from splitting apart ordinary cooking cloves, and the shallots are from the previous year's crop (the originals I received from a gardening friend in Iowa several years ago).

Peanuts A native of tropical South America, the peanut was originally introduced into Africa from Brazil. During colonial times, it was spread by traders from both Africa and Brazil into China, Japan, India, and North America. The manner in which the peanut is formed is intriguing. After the flower withers, a small pointed structure ("peg") remains behind. The peg, which contains the immature seeds, turns down and penetrates the soil to a depth of 1 or 2 inches, where it assumes a horizontal position and develops into a peanut.

There are basically two types of peanuts, those that run widely (Virginia) and those that bunch (Spanish). Many of the runner types have several peanuts in each pod, whereas the bunching types usually have only two. Almost all varieties require a long (100 to 150 days), warm growing season. If your season is long but cool, you may have difficulty producing a good crop of peanuts. Peanuts are one of those crops that are especially exciting to be around at harvest. It seems to thrill everyone from youngsters to senior citizens to see those clusters of peanuts hanging from the plants, and of course they enjoy eating them too!

Growing Essentials

¶ The area you select should be well drained and slightly sandy. Add organic matter as needed since it is important that the soil be loose so

103

that as pegs develop, they can push easily below ground.

¶ Add at least 2 to 3 pounds of 12–22–6 or similar fertilizer to each 10-by-10-foot plot. Peanuts use lots of calcium, and in the soil of some areas of the Great Plains, the absence of calcium is a problem. If you suspect that your soil calcium is low, increase it by adding lime.

¶ Plant seeds 1 inch apart in a trench 1 inch deep. Firm the soil over the seeds and water it thoroughly. The rows should be 12 inches apart.

¶ Plants should emerge in about 6 to 12 days. In my experience, germination is usually spotty, often only 40 to 60 percent. After the plants are about 1 inch tall, carefully thin them to about 10 to 12 inches between plants.

¶ When the plants are about 12 inches high, push the soil up around the base of the plants. This will help in the development of the pods.

¶ Provide adequate moisture to the plants during the growing season, and about every 4 weeks, fertilize them with a water-soluble fertilizer (for example, 15–30–15).

¶ The plants will be ready for harvest in the fall when they turn yellow. Use a garden fork and carefully pull up the entire plant. Gently shake off the dirt — there should be a cluster of peanuts hanging from the plant. Be sure the young gardeners are around to help at this stage!

¶ To cure the peanuts, hang the plants for at least 2 or 3 weeks in a warm, dry, well-ventilated area, such as a garage. The peanuts can then be stripped from the plants.

Pests and Diseases

Pests on peanuts are generally the same as those on beans and can be similarly treated.

Storing

After the peanuts have been dried, they can be prepared for storage. Place the unshelled peanuts in a wire basket in the oven at 475° to 500°F. Turn the oven off and allow it and the peanuts to cool. They will then be ready to eat or store.

Peanut Varieties I Have Tested

I have only tried one variety, Burpee Spanish 6216, with excellent results. It is very productive, and I had no problems with disease.

Peas Peas sometimes have a hard time making it to our family dinner table because one of our favorite ways to eat them is standing in the pea patch and shelling and eating them raw. It is hard to beat the sweet taste of peas fresh from the pod! Peas are a cool-season vegetable, and in my experience they are extremely tough in this respect. Although severe freezes may damage them, light frosts do not affect them seriously. I planted peas one season, saw them sprout, and then had two consecutive late-spring blizzards cover them with 5 feet of wet snow for 10 days. They recovered and went on to produce a great crop.

Peas grown by the home gardener are usually classified as one of two types: those with edible pods and seeds and those with edible seeds only. We plant both varieties, using the edible-pod type (for example, Sugar Snap and Oregon Sugar Pod) for stir-frying and the other type (for example, Sparkle and Early Perfection) for other recipes.

Growing Essentials

¶ Peas must be planted so they will mature and produce pods during cool weather. In Kansas, this means I always have my seeds in the ground at least 6 weeks (March 1–7) prior to the last frost date (April 20). If you plant them early, you can expect to harvest them from mid-May to mid-June. As a fall crop, peas can be started in early August (Colorado) or September (Kansas).

¶ I try to use varieties that are wind resistant because spring in the Great Plains is often windy. Wind-resistant varieties are usually shorter, but, more importantly, their stems seem to be stronger. I have found Oregon Sugar Pod, Little Marvel, Early Perfection, and Sparkle to be the most wind resistant.

¶ Excess nitrogen and potassium can damage pea roots. I apply a combination of 5–10–5 (2 pounds) and 0–20–0 (1 pound) for each 10-by-10-foot plot. Peas will grow in almost any kind of soil, but it should be relatively well drained.

Pests and Diseases

Several pests will attack peas, but the most serious in the Heartland seem to be mites or red spiders (early on) and various leaf-eating worms and grasshoppers (later on). Mites can be controlled with insecticidal soaps and pyrethrum sprays, and the other pests with *Bt* and pyrethrum as necessary. The most serious disease affecting peas in the Heartland is downy mildew. This can be treated with Bordeaux mixture or avoided by selecting resistant varieties (for example, Oregon Sugar Pod).

Storing

Edible-pod type peas will keep for at least 4 to 8 weeks (incredibly, Oregon Sugar Pod keeps 4 to 6 months!) if you simply place them in a closed plastic container and store them at about 40° to 50°F. Shelled peas can be stored by freezing after blanching them in boiling water for 3 minutes. It is important to process shelled peas quickly since their flavor deteriorates more rapidly than other vegetables.

Pea Varieties I Have Tested
(my favorite,*; E, edible pod; I, inedible pod)

Early Perfection*,I	Productive and wind-resistant (older plants seem especially wind resistant)
Extra Early Alaska I	Does very poorly in wind but good otherwise
Little Marvel*,I	Very productive and wind resistant
Oregon Sugar Pod*,E	My favorite for stir-frying; very productive; resistant to wind as well as mildew diseases
Sparkle*,I	Productive and wind resistant (seedlings and young plants seem especially wind resistant)
Sugar Snap E	Very productive
Thomas Laxton I	Does very poorly in wind but otherwise good

Peppers Although the pepper is certainly not the principal vegetable in many gardens, it would be hard to imagine any garden without at least one plant. Colorful and productive, this relative of the tomato and eggplant produces fruits that are usually hollow, not fleshy. Peppers, of course, are widely grown and cultivated by many gardeners for the "hot" flavor they add to such favorites as chili, but equally large numbers of gardeners grow the many sweet peppers that are available for salads, pickle relishes, and the like. The hot or sweet taste of a pepper is determined

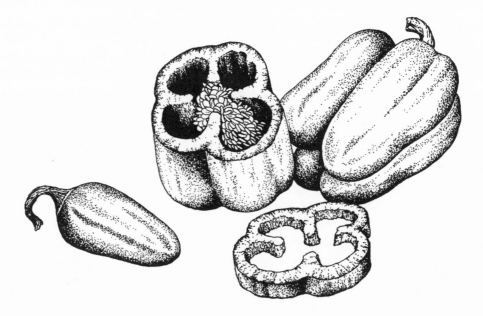

by the amount of capsaicin in the cells lining the wall of the fruit and in the seeds. Capsaicin causes cells of the body that are exposed to it to experience a hot or burning sensation. Relying on this fact, at least one foot powder containing ground hot peppers is marketed in sporting magazines as a foot-warming powder!

Growing Essentials

I use the same basic techniques for growing peppers as I do for eggplants, although peppers are not as tolerant of drought. The following tips for growing peppers have worked especially well for me.

¶ Start your plants about 7 to 8 weeks before you plan to set them in your garden (if I don't use Wallo'Waters, I plant 2 weeks after the last frost date). Use the same starting mix, trays, and transplanting techniques used for eggplants.

¶ Peppers respond especially well to extra heat and protection from the wind in the spring. I provide for both these needs by planting my transplants into Wallo'Waters 4 to 6 weeks prior to the last frost date. Wallo'Waters may be removed once the day- and nighttime temperatures remain quite warm (for example, in central Kansas, this would be about July 1), but I sometimes leave them on throughout the season as wind and hail protection. To keep the top open, I put a circular wire cage about 12 to 18 inches in diameter and 18 inches tall inside of them.

¶ Be sure that you place your plants 2 to 3 feet apart in a sunny part of your garden. If there is too much shade, your plants will produce lots of leaves and few peppers. Be careful not to overfeed your plants, especially with high-nitrogen fertilizers, as this also may result in plants with lush foliage and few fruits.

Pests and Diseases

I've never had many problems with pests and diseases bothering my peppers, although grasshoppers will sometimes eat holes in the leaves, and pill bugs and cutworms will occasionally eat holes in the fruits. Keeping the fruits off the ground will generally protect them from cutworms and pill bugs, and if the grasshoppers become a real menace, I treat the infestation with rotenone and pyrethrum. Nearly white to dark brown irregular spots of varying sizes may appear on the fruits. Caused by a combination of environmental stress (sunscald and blossom-end rot), bacteria (bacterial spot), fungi (blight, anthracnose, rot, and mildew) and viruses (mosaics), these have never become serious enough, in my experience, to require chemical treatment. I remove and discard affected peppers, and the problem usually corrects itself.

Storing

Peppers store relatively well if undamaged. I place freshly picked peppers in a loosely covered plastic container in a refrigerator at 40° to 50°F. Watch carefully for and discard any fruits that show signs of decay, especially from anthracnose. Most sweet peppers will keep this way for several weeks. I also freeze a few whole peppers in plastic bags for long-term storage. Hot peppers can be hung on a piece of string to dry in the sun. They can be kept almost indefinitely and used for decoration, although I prefer to grow new ones each year for eating.

Pepper Varieties I Have Tested (my favorite,*)

Standard Sweet Types	
Bell Boy*	Extremely productive and vigorous; always loaded with well-formed, flavorful fruits; my all-around favorite
Better Belle	Good overall but not as productive as Bell Boy or Jupiter
Big Bertha*	Robust plants and fruits
Crispy Hybrid	A prolific variety, but stems are not as strong as Bell Boy and so do not stand up well in wind
Jupiter*	Harvestable early and very productive; huge, blocky fruits
Keystone Giant	Productive
Ruby King	Productive
Tokyo Bell	Productive, but fruits are three-lobed and generally not as attractive as other bell types

I have also grown California Wonder.

Special Sweet Types	
Jung's Yellow Bell*	Robust producer of bright-yellow peppers; attractive blocky shape; great addition to or substitute for standard green bell peppers; great for freezer storage
Red Sweet Cherry*	Extremely productive; excellent for pickling; fruits not as sweet as standard green bell or yellow sweet banana
Yellow Sweet Banana*	Extremely productive and vigorous; sweet flavorful fruits; a nice substitute for bell types if banana-shaped peppers are desired

Hot Types	
Jalapeno*	Extremely productive and vigorous

Potatoes The potato is an ancient vegetable that traces its origins to Chile. The remains of tubers have been found in the food pits of ruins 13,000 years old, suggesting that the pleasures awaiting the palate from this delightful vegetable were well known historically. This fact was reemphasized much later during the Middle Ages when Gerard commented in his herbal that potatoes were "a meate for pleasure, equal in goodnesse and wholesomellesse vnto the same, being either rosted in the embers, or boyled and eaten with oyle, vinegar, and pepper, or dressed any otherway by the hand of some cunning in cookerie" — a testimonial that has truly stood the test of time! I usually plant 3 or 4 varieties of potatoes in my garden, including bakers and boilers, early and late types, and reds and whites. We enjoy eating new potatoes, so planting a number of different varieties insures that we'll have plenty when we want them. I simply can't imagine an early summer without new potatoes!

Growing Essentials

In my experience, potatoes are relatively easy to grow, although, as one might suspect from a vegetable with such a long history, the differences in varieties are pronounced. As a result, even though methods for growing them are relatively uniform, variety selection for an area is important for good success. I have found that the following steps work well for growing potatoes in the Heartland.

¶ Prepare the soil by adding lots of organic matter. This will help to lower the pH (potatoes are less likely to develop scab in slightly acidic soil) and increase the moisture-holding capacity of the soil.

¶ Fertilize the area to be planted with a combination of a superphosphate (0–20–0) and standard-balanced (for example, 8–10–8) fertilizers. I usually put 1½ to 2 pounds of each in a 10-by-10-foot area. As with most root crops, the additional phosphorus will promote the development of a healthy root system, resulting in well-formed potatoes.

¶ If at all possible, obtain certified potatoes for planting. Usually these are available in the early spring at greenhouses and supermarkets. I try to purchase the smallest potatoes (about golfball size), since I prefer to plant the whole potato. However, if all of the seed potatoes are quite large, I cut them into pieces that have at least 3 eyes. Potatoes should be cut into pieces about 2 days before planting. The cut side will dry somewhat and the piece will be less susceptible to rot. I have experimented with the small, scalloped eyes that are sold through many seed catalogs, but over a season they do not produce as well as the small whole potatoes.

¶ For a strong start, keep your seed potatoes in a warm place for at least 2 weeks prior to planting so they can begin to sprout.

¶ Plant your whole potato or piece (cut side down) in a hole 3 to 4 inches deep. Cover with soil and water thoroughly. I try to plant my potatoes about 4 weeks prior to the last frost date. Plants should be 12 inches apart in rows 18 to 24 inches apart.

¶ After your plants are about 6 inches tall, mound the soil around the plant until only the top shows. Then surround the small hills with mulch (grass clippings or straw). Treating the young plants this way will insure that the tubers formed later at the base of the plant reach maximum development.

¶ Keep the soil around your plants moist but not wet. Over the years, I have found that when potatoes are given generous amounts of water, they will often develop many small tubers, whereas if they are allowed to dry out too often, they develop a poor crop of tubers. I have had my best luck by simply deep soaking the potato patch at least once each week (less if rainfall is sufficient).

¶ Every 3 or 4 weeks, I fertilize my potatoes with a water-soluble fertilizer such as Miracle-Gro.

¶ New potatoes can be dug and used about 80 to 90 days after planting. Those to be stored should be allowed to grow for an additional 30 to 60 days, or until the tops die.

Pests and Diseases

The most consistent pest of potatoes is the Colorado potato beetle; the plants have usually barely emerged from the ground when I spot my first beetle. I religiously examine my plants at this stage and crush beetles I find as well as their orange egg masses on the bottom of the leaves. Many times, an early infestation can be controlled by careful handpicking. Since this pest is most common in early and midspring, controlling it at this time can help to prevent serious outbreaks later. When the plants become too large to handpick for beetles, or when I see larval stages on the leaves, I treat my plants very effectively with rotenone.

Colorado potato beetles can also be treated with *Bacillus thuringiensis* var. *San Diego,* which is sold as M-1 or Trident. Other pests that occasionally cause problems are psyllids, leafhoppers, grasshoppers, and tomato hornworms. The most serious disease I have experienced with potatoes is blight, but even when it killed my plants early, I still harvested a respectable crop. Blight can be prevented by planting resistant varieties. If the disease is present, the plants can be treated with Bordeaux mixture.

Storing

After digging up my potatoes, I carefully (so their skins are not damaged) wash them (with chlorinated water if available) to remove all dirt that might harbor bacteria that cause problems in storage. It is especially important to do this immediately if the clay content in your soil is high, since if left to dry, such soil is virtually impossible to remove without damaging the skin of the potato. After allowing the potatoes to thoroughly dry out of the sun, I store them in vinyl-coated, collapsible fish baskets sold in many stores. These allow the potatoes to be hung well off the ground and permit air circulation among the tubers. Potatoes should be stored in a cool (40 to 50°F if possible), dark place such as an unheated basement.

Potato Varieties I Have Tested
(my favorite,*; R, red; W, white; season — E, early; M, mid; L, late; B, boiler; K, baker)

Kennebec*,W,L,K	Excellent overall
Norgold*,W,E,K	Excellent overall
Red LaSoda*,R,M,B	Excellent overall; very attractive and tolerant of high temperatures
Red Norland*,R,E,B	Good overall, does not recover well from hail damage
Red Pontiac*,R,M,B	Excellent overall; a vigorous, very productive variety; recovers well from hail damage
Viking*,R,E,B	Harvestable extra early and very productive; great for new potatoes that are delicious boiled or mashed

I have also grown Early Ohio W,E,B, Norchip W,E,B, Mayfair W,M,B,K, and White Cobbler W,E,B,K.

Pumpkins At least two holidays, Halloween and Thanksgiving, would simply not be the same without the pumpkin. Can you imagine children and trick or treating without carved pumpkin faces, or turkey and dressing not followed by fresh pumpkin pie with a generous topping of whipped cream? The availability of productive bush pumpkins means even the smallest gardens have the space for at least one plant.

Growing Essentials
I use essentially the same techniques for growing pumpkins as for cantaloupe. These additional tips apply specifically to pumpkins.
¶ Children love pumpkins, and you can provide them with a special thrill by letting them make designer ones. If they write or draw anything on a pumpkin when it is immature, breaking the surface as they do, scar tissue will duplicate on the mature pumpkin what they have scratched. Have them write their names or draw a smiley face or goblin; they'll have their own designer pumpkins at Halloween.
¶ Harvest pumpkins when they are mature, usually after the vines have begun to wither and before the first hard frost or freeze.

Pests and Diseases

The pests and diseases of pumpkins are the same as those for squash. Treat them similarly.

Storing

Mature pumpkins should keep for 2 to 3 months if they are stored in a cool, dry area, such as a basement. Also, in short-season areas, well-developed green pumpkins can be picked and kept at room temperature to ripen slowly.

Pumpkin Varieties I Have Tested (my favorite,*)

Autumn Gold*	Pumpkins are orange from the beginning; a great variety if you need one early for a county fair
Big Max	Very susceptible to wilt
Spirit Hybrid*	Bush type; vigorous producer of several well-formed pumpkins on each plant; excellent size for jack-o'-lantern carving
Sugar*	Excellent for pies, and stores well; will ripen readily if picked green

Radishes　My mother-in-law loves to eat radishes. In fact, her favorite bedtime snack is a sandwich of sliced radishes on white bread. I can't guarantee that you'll like radish sandwiches, but I'm sure almost everyone has eaten and enjoyed radishes in some manner. Radishes are a sure sign of

Did You Know?
Stomata and Transpiration

The Beautiful

Most gardeners assume that the bulk of the organic substance in the broccoli head or tomato they pick and enjoy at the table is derived from water and/or nutrients in the soil. Actually, this is far from the truth as a Belgian doctor named Jan Baptista von Helmont showed more than 300 years ago. In a rather simple but ingenious experiment, he planted a tree weighing a few pounds in a container with 200 pounds of soil. He grew the tree for several years, adding only water, and then removed it and reweighed both the tree and the soil. Although the tree had increased its weight by more than 150 pounds, the soil had lost only a few ounces! Von Helmont proved that the soil was not the source of the organic matter in the plant, though he concluded incorrectly that it must have come from the water. We now know that most of the building blocks of plant matter come from the air, and specifically from carbon dioxide (CO_2), a gas we know is a waste product of decay or of the process of respiration. This waste gas is literally the breath of life for plants.

But how does carbon dioxide get into the plant from the atmosphere? You might guess that it is simply absorbed through the skin, or epidermis, of the plant. However, the surfaces of most plants are covered with a complex of fatty or waxy substances that forms a barrier (called a cuticle) to prevent the loss of water and consequently the rapid wilting and death of a plant. The cuticle also prevents the movement of gases into or out of a plant through the cells of the epidermis. You might then logically guess that the necessary carbon dioxide diffuses into the soil and is absorbed through the roots. Although this gas is found in the soil, there simply is not enough available to fulfill the needs of plants. Actually, plants obtain

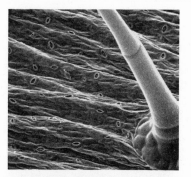

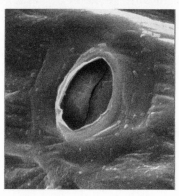

The surface of a green zucchini leaf magnified 200 times (top) exhibits numerous slit-shaped stomata. At even greater magnification (bottom, magnified 2,200 times) 2 guard cells which regulate the opening and closing of the stoma can be seen. Stomata are usually open during the day to allow carbon dioxide into the leaf for photosynthesis, but they close at night to prevent loss of water from the leaf through transpiration.

the carbon dioxide they need through minute breathing slits or pores in the leaves (sometimes also on the stems and roots) called stomata. These pores permit the exchange of vital gases between the atmosphere and the internal environment of the leaves. Each stomata is surrounded by specialized guard cells that control the opening and closing of the pores.

How are the stomata opened and closed? Surprisingly, not even professional botanists know all of the details. We do know that through a series of intricate reactions, the guard cells absorb large amounts of potassium (K) and water during the day and swell. This swelling causes the pores to open so gases can be exchanged. Unfortunately, there are problems associated with having, quite literally, holes in the leaf. The most serious is that water vapor is lost from the plant by evaporation through the stomata in a process called transpiration. Another problem is that disease organisms can enter the plant through an open stoma.

The Practical

The home gardener can do the following things to minimize the disadvantages of stomata on plants.

¶ If you overhead water with sprinklers, do so during the morning. This will moisten the soil and raise the humidity in the garden, thereby slowing transpiration during the hotter part of the day. It will also allow the surfaces of the leaves to dry off during the day. Sprinkling late in the day or at night creates a moist, warm environment in which fungal diseases thrive.

¶ When treating a plant for fungal infections, be sure that the lower surface of the leaf is thoroughly treated. Remember, the vast majority of stomata, through which the disease may be entering the plant, are found on the bottom of the leaves.

spring, although they are not as tolerant of the cold as some people believe. Nevertheless, they do their best during late spring, when the ground has warmed sufficiently, but the days and nights are still cool.

Growing Essentials

Although this vegetable is not difficult to grow, you'll have an abundance of tender, crisp radishes for your salads or whatever if you follow these tips.

¶ As with most vegetables, selecting the right variety can make a big difference. Although it is tempting to think that almost any radish will do, I have found quite the opposite to be true. Seeds are cheap, so experiment with different varieties until you find the one you like.

¶ Don't plant too early in the spring or too late in the fall. I usually plant about 4 to 5 weeks before the last frost and have had much success. By this time, the ground has warmed, but the days and nights remain cool. Generally, I plant succession crops about every 2 weeks until mid-May. Radishes planted after this time usually produce an abundance of tops and little else. My fall radishes are planted about August 1 (in the foothills of Colorado and South Dakota) or September 1 (in central Kansas) for a fall harvest.

¶ Fertilize the seed bed before planting. I use an 8–10–8, sometimes in combination with a 0–20–0, each at a rate of $1\frac{1}{2}$ pounds in each 10-by-10-foot area. Plant the seeds in rows 8 to 10 inches apart and, about 10 days after germination, thin the seedlings to about 1 inch apart. Approximately 2 weeks after the radishes emerge, I treat them once with a water-soluble fertilizer such as Miracle-Gro.

¶ Plant the radishes in the full sun and thin them. I have a gardening friend who told me he simply could not grow good radishes — that they all "go to tops." When he mentioned he was growing them under some trees, it was immediately apparent what his problem was: not enough sunlight. When radishes are planted in too much shade, they compensate for the reduction in sunlight (needed for photosynthesis) by putting their energy into producing larger leaves; as a result, the bottoms (roots) are small. Also, unthinned radishes, especially in less than full sunlight, will often produce small bottoms. I know that many folks do not thin their radish seedlings, but if you try thinning them to about 1 inch apart when they are 6 to 8 days old, I think you'll be amazed with the results at harvest.

¶ Water regularly and harvest before the radishes overmature or they may become hot and stringy or pithy.

114

Pests and Diseases

Radishes must taste really good to pests because the plants are barely above ground before they are attacked. The most common pest in my experience is the black flea beetle, a minute (pinhead size) pest that jumps when disturbed. This pest can rapidly devastate a row of radishes, but, fortunately, a dusting with rotenone quickly and effectively eliminates them. Other pests that chew on the roots of the radish include snails (especially in cooler areas of the Great Plains) and pill bugs, but the damage is usually not severe enough to require treatment with a pesticide.

Storing

Storing radishes for long periods and maintaining their quality is relatively easy. I harvest the radishes and immediately remove all but about 1/4 inch of the tops, leaving the root ends alone. I then wash them, being careful to remove all dirt, and air-dry them on a terry-cloth towel. It is very important that no excess moisture is on the radishes when you get ready to store them. I place the radishes in a sealed plastic container (a large margarine container works well) in the refrigerator. Radishes prepared and stored this way will keep for up to 4 months.

Radish Varieties I Have Tested
(my favorite,*; R, round; L, long; r, red; w, white)

Champion*,R,r	A great variety; heavy producer of mild, well-formed radishes that are slow to get pithy
Early Scarlet Globe R,r	A good, mild variety with average production
French Breakfast L,r	
Red Devil B R,r	A mild variety; smaller than Champion with a tendency to get fibrous quickly
Red Sparkler R,r	
White Icicle*,L,w	

Rhubarb Some books claim that rhubarb is a cool-season plant that does not grow well above 70°F. Don't believe it or you'll miss some delightful eating! I successfully grow rhubarb in west-central Kansas where temperatures above 100°F during the summer are not uncommon. Rhubarb will grow just about anywhere and anytime if you start it right and treat it well once it is established.

Rhubarb is grown for its leaf stalks, which are used in pies, jellies, crisps, and similar dishes. Anyone familiar with rhubarb knows there are few desserts that are more delicious than cold rhubarb crisp topped with whipped cream. Rhubarb has a tart to tart-sweet flavor and is

115

sometimes combined in recipes with other fruits, such as strawberries.

Growing Essentials

Rhubarb is a perennial plant that will provide a crop of leaf stalks for many years. If you follow these steps, you should have no trouble growing abundant rhubarb.

¶ Rhubarb develops from crowns that are divided into pieces for planting. Select pieces that are healthy and free of disease. If they are at all moldy, do not use them. I prefer to use cuttings I have taken from a plant in a friend's garden, or to purchase them at local greenhouses or stores where I can examine them closely.

¶ Rhubarb can be planted anytime from early spring to midsummer. One of the strongest plants in my garden is one that I planted in mid-July from a root given to me by my mother. The 100°F days initially caused all the leaves to die, but the plant recovered.

¶ Allow a 4-by-4-foot area for each plant. Till the soil thoroughly at least 18 inches deep, adding peat moss (at a rate of at least 2 cubic feet) and $^1/_2$ pound of 8–10–8 and $^1/_2$ pound of 0–20–0 fertilizers. Remember that your rhubarb will be in the same spot for several years, so this step is critical.

¶ Dig a hole about 6 to 8 inches across and about 10 inches deep. Spread a cup of 8–10–8 fertilizer evenly at the bottom. Cover with 3 to 5 inches of soil and firm the soil over the fertilizer.

¶ Place your crown piece so the top is just slightly below the surface. If it has leaves, do not remove them. Firm the soil over the piece, soak the soil, and apply a 1-inch layer of grass or straw mulch.

¶ Make sure the ground does not dry out. If the piece had leaves and they die don't worry — it doesn't mean the plant is dead.

¶ The piece should begin to produce new leaves within a month, probably sooner. When several new leaves have appeared, treat the plant with a water-soluble fertilizer (for example, 15–30–15) and again every 3 weeks thereafter.

¶ As your plants grow in the spring, remove any yellowish-white clusters of flowers and their stalks. If left to grow, these flower heads will drain energy from the plant, causing your plants to produce fewer leaves and stalks.

¶ Do not harvest any leaves the first year. In the second and succeeding years, you can harvest leaves throughout the summer, but don't take more than three-fourths of the leaves at any one picking. To harvest the leaves, grasp them near the base and pull them towards you. If you do this correctly, the bud at the base will remain behind, although two little leaflike growths (stipules) should be on the leaf stalk near the base. Remember that the leaves are poisonous — only the leaf stalks may be used.

¶ Each spring, fertilize the plants with ½ pound of 8–10–8 fertilizer worked into the soil near each plant. Fertilize the plants once a month thereafter with 2 gallons of a water-soluble fertilizer (for example, 15–30–15).

¶ Cover your plants each fall with a 4-to-6-inch layer of mulch.

¶ Every 5 or 6 years, you may need to divide your plants by taking a shovel in the early spring and digging up and removing half of the crown. Give it to a friend or plant it somewhere else in your garden. The half that is left behind will continue to grow.

Pests and Diseases

In my experience, rhubarb is most severely affected by cutworms, which damage the new leaves, and by rhubarb curculios, which burrow into the stalks. Both of these pests can be handpicked or dusted with rotenone. Grasshoppers also will sometimes chew on the leaves. Downy mildew may affect plants but usually only at the end of the season; in poorly drained areas, I have lost plants to bacterial or fungal rot of the roots.

Storing

Rhubarb stores well both fresh and frozen. Stored in a sealed plastic container at 40° to 50°F in a refrigerator, leaf stalks should keep for several weeks. To freeze rhubarb, simply cut the stalks into 1-inch sections, seal them in plastic freezer bags, and place them in the freezer. Frozen rhubarb will keep for 6 to 8 months.

Rhubarb Varieties I Have Tested

The rhubarb I grow was a gift from my mother, and I have no idea what variety it is. I suspect it is Valentine.

Squash Squash originated in the Americas — summer types in Central America and Mexico, winter types in South America. They were widely used by American Indians before being introduced into Europe during the Middle Ages. Every garden should include at least one squash. As prolific as they are, they make a great confidence builder for both beginning and master gardeners; their phenomenal productivity is legend. Just ask anyone who has ever raised green zucchini!

Few vegetables other than squash are characterized by a variety wide

117

enough to suit any gardener's desires. Those raised most commonly in home gardens are generally divided into three types: summer squash, winter squash, and pumpkins. Summer squash are eaten before they have ripened. Winter squash, by contrast, are eaten only after they have reached maturity, although there are some forms, such as Jersey Golden Acorn, that can be eaten while still immature. Pumpkins are typically orange at maturity and are used for baking pies or making jack-o'-lanterns (see the section on pumpkins, in this chapter).

Squash sometimes are accused of being tasteless but I believe this is a "bum rap," probably begun by people who have eaten zucchini squash only after the vegetables have been allowed to reach the proportions of a boxcar. Actually, squash are quite tasty, and there are varieties that can be prepared in almost any manner: summer types sliced in salads, deep-fried, or steamed with tomatoes, peppers, and onions; winter types baked with sausage, brown sugar and butter; and so on.

Growing Essentials

Squash are grown much like cantaloupe but with these additional tips.

¶ In warm soils, germination usually occurs in 4 to 5 days. It may take as long as 3 weeks if the soil is cool. As seeds are germinating, try to keep the soil moist but not wet. This helps prevent the loss of seedlings to damping-off.

¶ Do not trim the tips of the vines as you do with cantaloupe.

¶ Don't be surprised in cooler areas of the Great Plains if your plants don't really start growing and setting fruit until the hotter days of July arrive. (If your squash are flowering heavily but not setting any fruit, see Did You Know? Pollen, in this chapter.)

¶ With summer types, be sure to harvest the squash when they are 5 to 7 inches long. This is essential for making the squash more flavorful and tender and for stimulating the plant to produce more fruit. The exception would be green zucchini that are being grown to several pounds so they can be shredded and used for bread and cake or for long-term storage.

¶ After your plants have begun to set fruit, fertilize each plant at least once a week with 1 gallon of a water-soluble fertilizer (for example, 15–30–15).

¶ You might try growing some small ornamental gourds for decoration or for children and adults to paint on. However, many of these varieties are vigorous growers, and can become quite weedy. They also are generally very productive, as a gardening neighbor-friend once demonstrated to me after I made an off-color remark one evening about his gardening abilities. I awoke the next morning to find nearly 50 small, tan dipper gourds littering my neatly trimmed fescue lawn!

¶ At the end of the season, do not put diseased vines on your compost pile or till them into the soil. Get rid of them — if possible, by burning.

Pests and Diseases

Summer squash, with their tender-skinned rinds, are especially prone to damage by squash bugs, particularly when numerous immature ones settle on a single fruit. Control these by regularly handpicking, dusting with sabadilla or rotenone, spraying with pyrethrum, or enclosing the fruits in bags (paper or nylon hose). Squash vine borers will cause vines to wilt as will some bacterial and fungal wilt diseases. During hot weather, powdery mildews regularly attack my plants, so I am especially alert to small, round, fuzzy white spots on the leaves which reveal the disease's presence. When treated early, mildews are fairly easy to control with Bordeaux mixture, but if you wait, your plants may be too weak to survive. Plant resistant varieties whenever possible.

Storing

Summer squash. Most summer squash can be stored for only a short period, usually less than 2 weeks. I store mine in a refrigerator at 40° to 50°F. Some varieties that have been allowed to reach maturity (for example, Black Eagle green zucchini at 5 to 8 pounds) will keep for 4 to 9 months if placed so they are not touching each other in a box in a dark, well-ventilated, cool (50° to 65°F) spot, such as a basement.

Winter squash. Don't worry if you're one of the majority of home gardeners who do not have an elaborate root cellar to store their squash and other vegetables. Simply put your acorn or other winter squash in a dry, well-ventilated spot in your basement or garage. As long as the temperatures do not rise above 65°F or fall below freezing the squash should keep for 4 to 6 months. Be sure to either use promptly or discard any squash that show signs of deterioration, such as soft spots.

Squash Varieties I Have Tested (my favorite,*; B, bush type)

Summer	
Black Eagle Zucchini*,B	Productive and mature fruits store extremely well; excellent for use in bread recipes
Black Italian Zucchini*,B	Productive but do not store well
Bonita F1B	Good overall
Caserta*,B	Very productive and great flavor
Daytona CrookneckB	Productive yellow type

Early Prolific Straightneck[B]	Yellow type; very susceptible to soil fungi
Golden Eagle*,[B]	Very productive and great flavor
Marrow White Bush F1*,[B]	Very productive and great flavor; resistant to squash bugs
Sunburst Hybrid[B]	Yellow, scalloped fruits
Winter	
Mooregold	Bright-orange flesh
Ponca Butternut*	Harvest 30 to 45 days after fruits have set
Table Queen Acorn*	Very productive and stores well; excellent flavor; harvest when the spot on the side against the ground is bright orange, usually about 45 to 60 days after fruits set
Special	
Spaghetti*	Very productive and stores well; good flavor; very susceptible to mildews; can be harvested about 25 to 35 days after fruits set

I have also grown Jersey Golden Acorn[B] and Table King[B].

Strawberries Gerard indicated in his herbal that some of the "vertues" of strawberries were that they are "good against the passion of the heart, reuiuing of the spirits, and making the heart merry." I can't think of better reasons for growing this delightful plant, except perhaps the mouth-watering strawberry pie that my wife makes each spring. A strawberry patch should be a requirement in every garden. Strawberries grown in the garden are based on two wild varieties native to the Americas. Ironically, it was a Frenchman who first allowed the two species to hybridize, resulting in the garden strawberries we know today. Further development of these hybrids resulted in hundreds of cultivars. Many of these cultivars are highly adapted to certain environmental conditions, an important point to remember in selecting a variety for your garden.

There are essentially two types of cultivars based on their fruiting habits. The spring- (or June-) bearing type, which I prefer, depends on the short days of fall (not spring) to stimulate the development of flower buds that will open and produce fruit the next spring. The second type, called ever-bearing, flowers throughout the growing season. All strawberries require a dormancy period during which they must be subjected to a certain amount of chilling to stimulate growth and flowering the next spring.

Growing Essentials
The First Year
¶ Strawberries require a rich, well-drained soil for optimal development and do not do well in tight clay soils. Prepare a 10-by-10-foot plot by

tilling in 4 cubic feet of compressed peat moss. Then raise the bed slightly by placing redwood 2 x 4s around it. Spread 2 pounds of 8–10–8 and 1 pound of 0–20–0 fertilizers over the plot and work them into the upper 6 inches.

¶ Be sure that the plants you are going to use are healthy and free of disease. If they are moldy or look unhealthy, throw them away. If you start with diseased plants, you will have poor luck.

¶ Dig your holes so the roots of the plant can be spread slightly, and so they will extend at least 2 or 3 inches down into the soil. Holes should be 18 inches apart in all directions.

¶ Put the plant in the hole and soak the roots with a water-soluble fertilizer (for example, 15–30–15). Let the liquid drain from the hole and fill the hole around the plant with soil. Place the plant so the root-leaf junction is at soil level; if the crown is too deep or too exposed, the plant will often die. Water each plant again with about 1 quart of the water-soluble fertilizer.

¶ Mulch the plant to keep the soil moist. I prefer about 1 inch of grass clippings or straw.

¶ After about 5 or 6 weeks, the plants will begin to form runners. Direct these into the empty space in the square formed between 4 of the original, or parent, plants. At the end of each runner an offspring plant will develop. By gently pushing this plant into the ground, you can insure that it will root at the proper place. Allow only the parent plants and the one offspring plant to grow in each square. Remove all other runners for the rest of the season, as well as any flowers that appear on the parents of offspring plants the first year.

¶ Be sure not to allow your plants to dry out during the summer. Fertilize the plants every 3 weeks throughout the growing season with about 1 quart each of a water-soluble fertilizer (for example, 15–30–15).

¶ In the fall, mulch the plot with several inches of straw. This will not prevent the strawberries from chilling (a requirement for fruit production), but it will prevent the bed from warming too early in the spring. Remove the mulch in the spring so the plants can resume growth. However, remember that if the strawberries resume growth and begin flowering too soon in the spring, the flowers may be damaged or destroyed by late frosts, and your strawberry crop will be very small.

Second and Subsequent Years

¶ Remove any mulch from your bed about 3 weeks before the last frost date and water the soil if necessary. If freezing temperatures threaten, cover your plants to prevent damage to the developing flowers.

Did You Know?

Transport Systems

The Beautiful

Throughout every garden plant is an intricate and remarkable network of cells — the vascular system — that serves as a transport system in plants. This system, which extends from the tips of the roots to the edges of the leaves, guarantees that minerals and water from the soil and sugars produced in the leaves during photosynthesis are available to every cell in the plant. The cells in this system are organized into two groups or tissues: the xylem, which conducts water and minerals up, and the phloem, which conducts sugars produced during photosynthesis primarily down.

In all garden plants, the xylem contains a great number of structures called vessels. A vessel consists of numerous cells connected end to end to form a long tube — like barrels stacked on top of one another. The cells in this tube are dead and hollow when functional, and the walls blocking each end are gone. Thus, as I tell my beginning botany students, a vessel is essentially like a pipeline. The cells in this pipeline are usually quite rigid and are partially responsible for the "woody" nature of many plants. Like a pipeline, these vessels are extremely efficient at moving large volumes of water throughout the plant body.

The vessels function well as long as sufficient water is available in the soil. Even during periods of intense heat, when loss of water at the end of the pipeline (through the stomata by evaporation) may be the greatest, the xylem effectively supplies plant cells with enough water to survive. However, during periods of drought, the xylem may not be able to supply enough to the main body cells (parenchyma) of

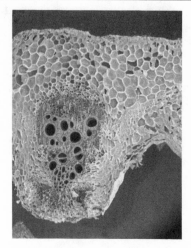

the plant; so these cells lose water and collapse like dried-up peas, and the plant wilts. If left in this wilted condition long enough, the plant will die.

Sometimes disease can affect the xylem and cause the death of a plant, as in the case of wilt diseases in tomatoes (caused by fungi) and vine crops (caused by bacteria). For example, in cucumber wilt, a bacterium or fungal spore is introduced into vessels by infected insects, such as a cucumber beetle or squash bug, as they feed on the plant. The bacteria or fungi multiply rapidly in the vessels, eventually plugging them and preventing the movement of water. As a result, the plant wilts and dies.

Closely associated with the xylem is the other transport tissue in plants, called the phloem. The phloem is responsible for moving sugars to every cell in the plant. These sugars are needed by the cells to nourish the energy processes that keep cells alive. Like the xylem cells, the phloem cells are connected end to end into long tubes (sieve tubes). Unlike xylem cells,

the phloem cells are living at maturity and retain walls at the ends of each cell. Organic food substances, such as sugars, are moved from cell to cell through areas in the phloem cells called sieve plates. These plates have a number of holes or pores that control the exchange of materials between cells. Since the phloem cells are not hollow, the sugars move more slowly through the plant than water does.

The Practical

To understand transport systems in plants, keep these things in mind.

¶ Be especially alert to the problems that wilt-infected sucking and chewing insects can cause. If you can keep these insects away from your plants, you can prevent wilt diseases.

¶ Wilt disease in one plant will not affect other plants in your garden unless the disease is carried to them by an infected insect. Wilt diseases cannot be treated, so as soon as you notice an infected plant, immediately remove and destroy it, preferably by burning. Do not throw it on a compost pile.

¶ In especially hot weather, the water transport systems of some plants, such as broccoli, cannot keep up with water loss through the leaves, and these plants will sometimes wilt, even though soil moisture is adequate. Don't confuse this physiological wilting with wilting caused by disease.

¶ Water must enter the vessels through the roots. Therefore, if you encourage the development of a deep root system in your plants by deep soaking rather than by overhead sprinkling, the whole transport system will be more tolerant of drought. You will also save water and money.

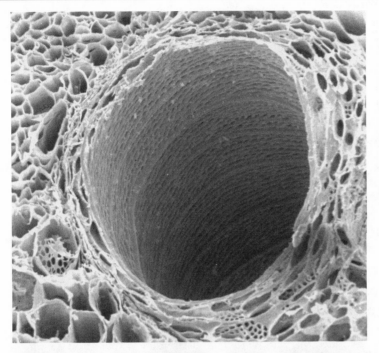

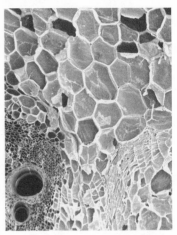

These micrographs show the "plumbing" inside a green zucchini stem. A section through a stem vein (opposite page, magnified 20 times) shows a number of round, black holes. These holes are the tubes, or vessels (upper left, magnified 590 times), that carry large amounts of water and minerals into the tissues of the squash plant. One of these tissues, the parenchyma, consists of large, angular gray cells (upper right, magnified 70 times) that store water. When a squash plant is deprived of water, these cells collapse and the plant wilts.

Food in the form of sugars is manufactured in the leaves during photosynthesis and carried throughout the plants by sieve tubes. These tubes are composed of cells with plates at each end full of small holes (lower left, magnified 650 times). If a sieve-tube cell is injured, as those in the photograph were during preparation, the cell protects itself by depositing a mass of material, called a slime plug, over the plate. These plugs prevent further loss of nutrient sugars from the injured cells.

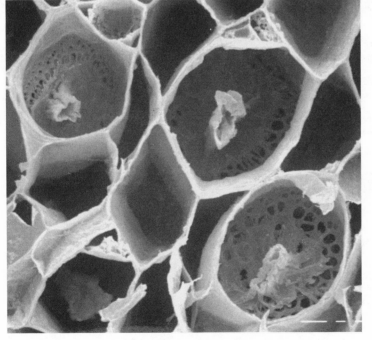

123

¶ With June-bearing varieties, the first flowers should appear within 3 to 4 weeks, and the berries should be ready for harvest about 5 weeks later. A bed can generally be harvested for about 2 to 3 weeks. Ever-bearing varieties will produce flowers and fruits throughout the growing season, although they are most productive during cool periods.

¶ After the harvest is finished, the bed must be renewed. This is done by completely removing and discarding the original plants. Last year's offspring plants now become the parents for the next year. Follow the same procedure used the first year for developing new offspring plants.

¶ After thinning the plants, rake in 2 to 3 pounds of a 5–10–5, 8–10–8, or similar fertilizer into the bed around the new parent plants. Water thoroughly and deep soak weekly or as needed.

¶ The remaining steps are identical to those used the first year (thinning runners, fertilizing, and so on). Every 4 years, tear out all of the plants in your bed and begin with new plants.

Pests and Diseases

The two insects that most damage strawberries are leaf-roller worms, which feed on the leaves, and pill bugs (roly-polies), which damage the berries. The worms can be controlled by crushing them with your hands (the leaves pulled together by their webs are easy to spot), and the pill bugs can be treated with rotenone. Viral diseases that attack strawberries are best controlled by planting virus-free stock, and fungal diseases that infect strawberries are best controlled by a combination of good drainage and selecting resistant varieties. Birds, especially robins and grackles, like strawberries, and you may need to cover them with a net toward harvest time.

Storing

Fresh strawberries do not store well for long periods. They should be air-dried and placed in a refrigerator at 40° to 50°F shortly after they are picked and then used as soon as possible. They can be sliced and frozen in some sugar water and their own juices for long-term storage.

Strawberry Varieties I Have Tested

(my favorite,*; S, spring-bearing; E, ever-bearing)

Ogallala*,E	Good productivity and very sweet
Surecrop*,S	A vigorous variety with large, tasty berries

I have also grown Gurney's Ever-bearing[E] and Ostara[E].

Sweet Potatoes Although they are called potatoes, sweet potatoes are not related to standard red and white potatoes. In fact, standard potatoes are in the

124

plant family that includes tomatoes and peppers, whereas sweet potatoes are in the same family as bindweed and morning glory! About the only similarity that standard and sweet potatoes have is that we harvest underground portions for use. Even then, there is a difference, because the standard potato is actually an underground stem, but the sweet potato is a tuberous root.

Growing Essentials

¶ Sweet potatoes are originally a subtropical plant and do best in warm areas in a rich soil. Prepare a 10-by-10-foot plot by tilling in 4 cubic feet of compressed peat moss and adding 2 pounds of 8–10–8 and 1 pound of 0–20–0 fertilizers to the upper 6 inches.

¶ Sweet potatoes are planted from sprouts grown from the top of a stored sweet potato. Sprouts can be purchased at a greenhouse or you can grow your own from a sweet potato purchased in a grocery store. If you grow your own, however, you probably won't know the variety. To grow your own, simply leave a sweet potato in a warm, well-lit place until it begins to sprout at the stem end. Bury the sweet potato three-quarters (stem end up) into a container of potting soil and then water it. Keep the soil moist and fertilize it about every two weeks with a water soluble fertilizer. After about 2 or 3 months, a number of sprouts will have developed, and they can be removed and planted.

¶ Sweet potatoes thrive on heat, so don't rush their planting. I always wait until at least 1 month after the last frost date to plant so that I am certain the soil is warm and that both the day- and nighttime temperatures will be warm (preferably above 60°F).

¶ When planting, I dig a hole into which I place the sprout to the depth of its first leaves, allowing 18 to 24 inches between each sprout. I then fill the hole with a water-soluble fertilizer, allow it to soak in, fill the hole with surrounding dirt, and firmly pack it around the sprout. I soak everything again with fertilizer.

¶ Be sure to keep the soil around your plants moist during the growing season. After the plants have begun to spread 12 inches or more, I apply an organic mulch, such as grass, to keep the soil moist and prevent weed growth.

¶ About once a month, apply 1 gallon of a water-soluble fertilizer (for example, 15–30–15) at the base of each plant.

¶ Sweet potatoes can be harvested about 90 to 120 days after planting. The tubers develop erratically under individual plants, so don't be surprised if you have one plant with poorly developed tuberous roots and another with well-developed ones.

Pests and Diseases

I have had no serious problems with pests on sweet potatoes. Occasionally, cucumber beetles and Mexican bean beetles will eat holes in the leaves, and during hot weather, mites will sometimes attack them, but none of these pests seems to cause much damage. If they do, a combination of rotenone and insecticidal soap effectively controls them.

Storing

Although sweet potatoes can be used immediately, many gardeners like to store some. To store sweet potatoes, you should cure them in a warm (75° to 85°F), moist area for about 2 weeks. Be careful not to bruise the roots during harvesting since this will shorten their potential storage life. Properly harvested and cured sweet potatoes will keep for 2 to 4 months.

Sweet Potato Varieties I Have Tested (my favorite,*)

Centennial	A spreading productive variety; good yields and harvestable slightly earlier than Porto Rico
Porto Rico*	A vigorous bush type that produces lots of 1-to-4-pound sweet potatoes; great for small gardens

Tomatoes Undoubtedly, the tomato is one of the best-loved and most popular vegetables among gardeners, but this has not always been the case. Gerard indicated that tomatoes, or apples of love, "yeeld very little nourishment to the bodie" and, further, that these apples of love were "corrupt." Little did he know that this vegetable would later be raised and praised by tens of millions of home gardeners in nearly every environment. Interestingly, Gerard did note that some people in his day "does eat the Apples with oile, vinegar, and pepper mixed together for sauce to their meat." Apparently, some gardeners were well ahead of their time!

I've always thought that tomatoes were amazingly easy to grow, although getting them to produce fruit has sometimes been a challenge, especially during hot, windy summer months. In addition, there is a whole chorus of diseases and insects waiting in the wings to pounce on the unwary gardener and his plants. Nevertheless, the absolutely unmatched flavor of home-grown and vine-ripened tomatoes is enough to encourage any gardener to risk the potential pitfalls awaiting his or her efforts. Indeed, tomato plants are such prolific growers that short of a major disease such as fusarium, some success can always be expected. Even Gerard noted this great productivity in his seventeenth century herbal when he indicated that "I haue in the hottest tine of Sommer cut away the superflous branches from the mother root, and cast them away carelesly in the allies of my garden, the which haue growne as fresh where I cast them, as before I did cut them off." Little wonder that tomatoes are so loved and admired.

Growing Essentials

If you'd like to grow tomatoes, I believe you'll have much success if you follow these steps.

¶ Start your plants about 3 to 4 weeks prior to the last frost date (10 to 12 weeks if you are planning to use Wallo'Waters; see step 5) so they are about 5 to 7 weeks old at transplanting. I usually try to have 6 to 10 different varieties in my garden each year.

¶ Plant seeds according to the general instructions, but fill each cubicle only halfway with starting mix. When the seedlings are about 3 inches

tall, fill the cubicles to the top with the mix. New roots will develop along the newly buried stem and, as a result, you will have young plants with stronger root systems. At about 3 weeks, I usually repot some of my young plants into larger containers. Quart or half-gallon waxed-paper milk or juice containers are great, but be sure to put drainage holes in the bottom.

¶ Tomatoes thrive in a healthy soil. In each 10-by-10-foot plot, add abundant organic matter and at least 4 pounds of an 8–10–8 or similar fertilizer. Avoid excess nitrogen and add calcium (with lime), if necessary, to prevent blossom-end rot.

¶ Unless you use Wallo'Waters, transplant to the garden about 2 to 3 weeks after the last frost date. When transplanting tomatoes, remove all but the uppermost two leaves and bury the length of stem below these leaves either vertically or horizontally in the soil (see pp. 16–17). Roots will develop along the entire length of the buried stem. Cover each transplant with a hotkap or similar device to protect it from the elements.

¶ For extra-early tomatoes, try transplanting into Wallo'Waters 1 to 2 months prior to the last frost date. These are the best protection devices I have ever used. They not only protect the transplant from wind, frost, hail, and snow but also warm the ground beneath the plant (encouraging a strong root system) and create a warm, favorable environment for plant growth inside the Wallo'Water. They must be set up about 1 week before the transplanting date to warm the soil.

¶ Situate your transplants so that your tomatoes are not bunched in a single area. I have found that this helps prevent or slow the spread of insects and diseases through the garden. Allow at least a 4-by-4-foot area for each plant.

¶ Tomato plants must be transplanted into an area where they will get at least 6 hours of direct sunlight each day. Any less and you will probably get lots of leaves and few or no tomatoes.

¶ About 2 months after transplanting, side dress each plant with about 1 cup of granular fertilizer (for example, 8–10–8). I usually apply 1 gallon of water-soluble fertilizer (for example, 15–30–15) every 2 weeks.

¶ Tomatoes with an indeterminate growth habit continue to grow and produce fruit throughout the season. These sprawl widely and need to have the support of large cages and/or trellises to keep the fruit off the ground. Determinate types do not grow throughout the season and usually look bushy. These do well either staked or in cages.

¶ Cracking in tomatoes is caused by sudden fluctuations in soil moisture during fruit growth and ripening, especially following periods of cool, rainy weather. Keep your soil moisture consistent by using mulches and a regular watering schedule.

¶ If you are one of those folks who have trouble getting their tomatoes to ripen, I have a couple of suggestions. Both involve putting stress on the plant so that it will hurry to complete its life cycle by ripening its fruit. First, you can simply stop watering your plants. I always tell my gardening friends that as long as the water keeps flowing, tomatoes will keep growing. Sometimes drying them up a bit is all that is needed to force ripening. If this doesn't work, take a shovel, place it 8 to 10 inches from the base of the plant, and cut the roots around half of the plant. Don't dig the roots; merely sever them by driving the shovel 10 to 12 inches into the ground. Using one or both of these suggestions should hasten ripening of your tomatoes.

If you follow the steps I've outlined, you'll have more tomatoes than you know what to do with, and won't that be terrible!

Pests and Diseases

I am convinced that tomatoes are as popular with pests and diseases as they are with gardeners. The pests you can expect to find most often on your plants and fruits will be worms (fruitworms; hornworms; and white grubs, often from June beetles), whiteflies, mites, psyllids, and grasshoppers. You will also probably see one of several diseases caused by various fungi, bacteria, and viruses. Worms can be controlled with *Bt,* the whiteflies and mites with insecticidal soap, and the grasshoppers with my special cocktail (see chapter 5). Many tomato diseases — for example, blight and leaf spot — can be controlled with Bordeaux mixture or sulfur, but some — for example, mosaic (virus) and fusarium and verticillium wilts (fungi) — can be controlled only by planting resistant varieties.

Storing

Unbruised or otherwise undamaged tomatoes will store fresh for 2 to 3 weeks in a refrigerator around 40° to 50°F. They should be kept dry and arranged in a single layer. If they are picked green, many tomatoes can be ripened over 2 to 5 weeks by keeping them where the temperature is 65° to 80°F. Be sure to leave the fruit stalk attached and to place the tomatoes in a single layer, unwrapped, in a covered box. Check them frequently and discard any fruits that show signs of mold. I have tried the Long-Keeper tomatoes, but have not found their taste to be worth the efforts of growing and storing them. We commonly store tomatoes for long-term use by freezing them whole. After we dip them in hot water, their skins slip off easily. We then add the tomatoes to any recipe calling for canned tomatoes — chili is one of our winter favorites. Tomatoes can also be readily canned. You should consult a book on canning for details.

Tomato Varieties I Have Tested (my favorite,*; H, hybrid; growth habits — I, indeterminate; D, determinate)

Avalanche*[H,I]	Resistant to fusarium wilt (F); great for mid- and late-season harvests
Baxter's Bush Cherry*[H,I]	Very productive
Better Boy*[H,I]	Resistant to F, to verticillium wilt (V), and to nematodes (N); good to great for midseason harvests; excellent flavor
Celebrity*[H,D]	Resistant to V, to fusarium wilt race 1 (F1) and race 2 (F2), to N, and to tobacco mosaic virus (T); good overall
Early Girl*[H,I]	Resistant to V; my favorite early type in all areas; somewhat acidic; very resistant to cracking
Jet Star*[H,I]	Great for mid- and late-season harvests; picked green, they ripen evenly
Red Cherry (large-fruited)*[I]	Excellent overall and prolific
Rushmore*[H,I]	Resistant to V and F; great for hot-summer areas
Super Fantastic*[H,I]	Resistant to V, F, and N; great for mid- and late-season harvests; produces truly fantastic results
Super Sioux*[H,I]	Excellent early-season harvest, especially in northern areas; ripens evenly in storage; great for cool-summer regions
Surprise*[H,I]	Resistant to V and F; very productive; great for midseason harvest; large fruits; great in hot, windy areas

I have also grown Beefmaster[H,I] (V,F,N), Better Girl[H,I] (V,F,N), Big Pick[H,I] (V,F,N,T), Burpee Early Pick[H,I] (V,F), Burpee Pixie[H,D] (F), Burpee Supersteak[H,I] (V,F,N), Champion[H,I] (V,F,N,T), Floramerica[H,I] (V,F1&2), Glamour[I], Golden Boy[H,I], Gurney Girl[H,I] (V,F,N,T), Homestead[D], Long Keeper[H,I], Park's Whopper[H,I] (V,F,N,T), President[H,D] (V,F,N,T), Quick Pick[H,I] (V,F,N,T), San Marzano[I], and Show Me[H,I].

My Favorite Recipes

Over the years, one of the most enjoyable aspects of home gardening has been eating the results of our labors. As every gardener knows, the taste of fresh home-grown vegetables is simply unmatched. Witness how we all wait anxiously for that first vine-ripened tomato or ear of sweet corn. Also, knowing exactly where the vegetables have come from and what chemical has or has not been used in their production enhances the enjoyment of eating them — as my mother-in-law said, "They are healthy eating." Finally, every gardener who has ever brought produce to the table understands the satisfaction, accomplishment, and pride one experiences when someone at supper comments on the delicious broccoli or sweet carrots from your garden!

To help you enjoy your home-grown produce, I offer some of my favorite recipes. Although seasonings are given for each, experiment to suit your own taste.

Garden Vegetable Salad
2 cups fresh chopped cabbage
$1/2$ cup grated carrots
$1^1/_2$ cups chopped celery
$1/2$ cup chopped onions
$1^1/_2$ cups chopped green (or yellow) bell pepper
$1/2$ cup chopped red pepper
$1/4$ cup white vinegar
$1/4$ cup sugar
dash of fresh ground black pepper

Combine all ingredients and mix thoroughly. Vinegar and sugar may be adjusted to taste. Refrigerate all day or preferably overnight before serving.

Diana's Fresh Spinach Salad

30 to 40 small spinach leaves, whole
2 hard-boiled eggs, sliced
4 to 6 green onions, sliced
1 orange, peeled and quartered
honey
bread croutons
1 small bottle of Italian dressing

Wash and pat dry spinach leaves. Drizzle leaves with small amount of honey and toss. Add eggs, onions, and orange sections. Toss and chill. Just before serving, add croutons and bottle of salad dressing.

Miracle Cucumbers

3 medium cucumbers, sliced thin
$\frac{1}{3}$ cup Miracle Whip
1 tablespoon vinegar
1 tablespoon sugar
salt, pepper, dill weed, and milk

Put cucumbers in a bowl and add salt, pepper, and dill weed to taste. Mix Miracle Whip, vinegar, and sugar and pour over cucumbers. Gradually add milk until ingredients reach a desirable consistency. Chill before serving.

Hot or Cold Squash Delight

3 immature summer or zucchini squash (3 to 6 inches)
2 to 3 large ripe tomatoes
1 large green pepper or 3 sweet yellow peppers
1 small onion or shallot

Wash vegetables and slice into a 10-inch teflon-coated frying pan. Add 3 tablespoons of water. A small amount of salt, pepper, and butter may be added if desired. Simmer covered over medium heat until squash is tender. May be eaten hot or chilled and served cold.

Fresh Cooked Beans

1 pound green snap beans
$^1/_2$ medium onion, or 3 shallots, chopped
3 strips uncooked bacon, cut up

Fill pot with water to cover all ingredients. Boil until beans are tender, drain, and season with butter, salt, and pepper to taste.

Scotty's Beets

6 to 8 lemon-sized beets
$^1/_4$ teaspoon lemon juice
$^1/_4$ cup butter
$^1/_4$ cup brown sugar

Beets: Boil beets until tender; peel and quarter them.
Sauce: Mix lemon juice, butter, and brown sugar in a small sauce pan and melt over medium heat. Put warm quartered beets in a small microwave dish and pour sauce over them. Serve immediately or heat in microwave for 30 seconds before serving.

Buttered Acorn Squash

1 acorn squash, halved
1 tablespoon butter
1 tablespoon brown sugar
1 tablespoon raisins

Combine butter and brown sugar in the cavity of the squash. Cook covered with aluminum foil in a conventional oven or in a microwave dish in a microwave oven until tender. Add raisins and cook for an additional 5 to 8 minutes in a conventional oven or 1 to 2 minutes in a microwave.

Zucchini-Tomato Beef Casserole

3 medium zucchini
1 pound ripe tomatoes, peeled
1 small onion or 3 shallots, chopped
1 pound ground beef
$\frac{1}{2}$ cup mushrooms
Worcestershire sauce

Wash squash and cut into bite-sized chunks. Boil with a little water until tender. Brown ground beef in a pan, add a small onion or a few shallots, and season to taste with salt, pepper, and Worcestershire sauce. When onion or shallots are tender, add tomatoes and mushrooms. Drain squash and add to beef mixture. Simmer 20 to 30 minutes. Top with bread crumbs and grated cheese and serve.

Ruby Jane's Yellow Squash Casserole

2 yellow squash, sliced
3 tablespoons dry rice
$\frac{1}{2}$ cup sour cream
grated cheese

Combine squash, rice, and sour cream in a casserole dish and add salt and pepper as desired. Cover with cheese (your choice) and bake at 350°F for 30 minutes.

Eggplant Lasagna

2 to 3 small to medium eggplants
spaghetti sauce, prepared
mozzarella cheese, sliced

Peel and slice eggplants. Salt and pepper slices and brown on both sides in a pan with a small amount of oil. Layer eggplant, your favorite spaghetti sauce, and cheese twice in a casserole dish. Bake uncovered at 350°F for 30 minutes until sauce bubbles.

Nadine's Strawberry Pie
Filling
4 cups whole strawberries
3 tablespoons dry strawberry Jell-O
1 cup sugar
2 tablespoons cornstarch
1 cup water

Cook sugar, cornstarch, and water together over medium heat until clear and thick. Remove from stove and stir in strawberry jello. Allow mixture to cool.

Crust (no roll)
$1/2$ cup cooking oil
2 tablespoons milk
$1 1/2$ cups flour
2 tablespoons sugar
1 teaspoon salt

Blend ingredients and pat with fingers into a 10-inch pie tin. Bake at 375°F for about 15 minutes. Allow crust to cool. After crust has cooled, put whole strawberries in crust and pour in cooled filling mixture. Serve with whipped topping.

Grandma T's Rhubarb Cream Pie
2 cups diced rhubarb
$1 1/4$ cups sugar
$1 1/2$ cups evaporated milk or coffee cream
2 egg yolks, well beaten
2 tablespoons margarine
2 tablespoons cornstarch

Melt margarine in pan. Add rhubarb and 1 cup of sugar and cook slowly over medium heat until rhubarb is tender. Combine remaining sugar, cornstarch, egg yolks, milk, and a pinch of salt. Add to rhubarb mixture and cook until thick. Pour into baked pie shell and top with meringue if desired. Bake 8 to 10 minutes at 400°F.

Grandma G's Blackberry Pie

huckleberries (enough to fill a pie crust)
1 cup sugar
1 can evaporated milk
2 tablespoons flour

Add huckleberries to a 10-inch pie crust until filled halfway. Mix sugar, evaporated milk, and flour and beat well. Pour over berries and bake for 40 to 45 minutes at 350°F until golden.

Aunt L's Carrot Cake

1 cup oil
2 cups sugar
3 eggs
2½ cups flour
1 teaspoon baking soda
1 teaspoon salt
2 teaspoons vanilla
1 teaspoon cinnamon
2 cups grated carrots
1 cup chopped walnuts or pecans
1 cup crushed, drained pineapple

Blend all ingredients in a bowl and pour in a greased 13-by-9-by-2-inch pan. Bake for 1 hour at 350°F.

Nancy's Sweet Potato Pie

3 medium sweet potatoes, peeled and cooked
1 can sweetened, condensed milk
1 stick butter
1 teaspoon cinnamon
½ teaspoon nutmeg
¼ teaspoon salt
2 eggs

Mix ingredients well and pour batter into uncooked pie shell. Bake at 350°F for 50 to 55 minutes.

Appendix 2 Flower Varieties
to Plant near Heartland Vegetable Gardens

Blanket Flower *(Gaillardia grandiflora).* A perennial that produces large, showy, reddish-orange, yellow-trimmed blossoms throughout the summer; very resistant to heat.

Blue Bedder Sage (Northrup King). A semi-hardy, vigorous perennial that is less compact than broad leaf sage (grows to 3 to 4 feet); produces abundant blue flowers from early summer through fall.

Broad Leaf Sage (Northrup King). An extremely hardy variety and a vigorous low bush that grows to 1 to 2 feet; produces abundant blue flowers in late spring; mantids like to lay egg cases on this plant's woody stems, but grasshoppers are also attracted to it.

Butterfly Milkweed *(Asclepias tuberosa).* Native to many areas of the Great Plains, this extremely hardy perennial produces a bright orange mass of flowers from early to late summer; best started from transplants, this milkweed takes 2 to 3 years to reach full development; does best in hot, dry, sunny areas where plenty of ground limestone has been added to the soil; attracts lots of ladybugs.

Marigolds An enormously popular flower with many gardeners, the marigold comes in a wide assortment of colors and sizes; very resistant to heat, it blooms from early summer to first frost and is a favorite hiding place for mantises. Be aware that mites also love marigolds.

Painted Daisy *(Pyrethrum roseum).* A perennial that produces large (2 to 3 inch wide) rose to crimson blossoms in early summer and later if it is trimmed.

Penstemon Like its relative the snapdragon, the penstemon is quite tolerant of the heat, but is also susceptible to rust disease; a true perennial, penstemon flowers from early through late summer in a variety of colors; it should be planted in well-drained areas.

Petunia A favorite annual in many gardens, this heat-resistant plant produces a wide variety of colorful blossoms from early summer to first killing frost.

Shasta Daisy (*Chrysanthemum maximum*). A perennial that is somewhat less hardy than the painted daisy; does best in well-drained areas.

Snapdragon Many heat-tolerant varieties; although often listed as an annual, snapdragons can be covered during the winter in milder areas of the Great Plains and treated as a perennial; produces multi-colored blossoms throughout the season if flower spikes are trimmed as they mature; look for rust-resistant varieties.

Sunflower A natural for Heartland gardens, the sunflower comes in several varieties that produce stunning 10-to-15-inch-wide flowers loaded with seeds either for eating or for using as birdseed.

Annotated Bibliography

Carrots Love Tomatoes (book, 226 pages). 1976. Storey Communications, Pownal, Vt. Information on companion planting.

Complete Vegetable Gardener's Sourcebook (book, 336 pages). 1989. Prentice-Hall Press, New York, N.Y. Excellent source for information on specific vegetable varieties.

Controlling Tomato Diseases (pamphlet, 12 pages). 1976. Government Printing Office, Washington, D.C., or local extension offices.

Directory of Seed and Nursery Catalogs (pamphlet, 14 pages). 1987. National Gardening Association, Burlington, Vt. Addresses for sources of seeds and garden products, including natural pesticides and biological controls.

Field Guide to Garden Pests (special magazine issue). Mother Earth News, American Country, v. 1, no. 2, May 1987. Excellent information on insects and companion planting.

Gardening (book, 431 pages). 1986. National Gardening Association, Burlington, Vt. A must for every gardener.

Harrowsmith Northern Gardener (book, 208 pages). 1982. Camden House Publishing, Camden East, Ontario. Many ideas for frost protection.

Identifying Diseases of Vegetables (book, 62 pages). 1983. Pennsylvania State University, Box 6000, University Park, Pa. Great color plates.

Insects and Diseases of Vegetables in the Home Garden (bulletin, 54 pages). 1980. Government Printing Office, Washington, D.C., or call local extension offices. Out of print but worth looking for.

Joy of Gardening (book, 365 pages). 1982. Garden Way Press, Troy, N.Y. Marvelous pictures and great basic information.

National Gardening Magazine (6 issues annually). National Gardening Association, Burlington, Vt. Beautiful color; very informative.

Organic Gardening (9 issues annually). Rodale Press, Emmaus, Pa. Much valuable information.

Pest Control in Vegetable Gardens (1982), *Wilt and Virus Diseases of Tomatoes* (1985), *Leaf and Fruit Diseases of Tomato* (1985), and other pamphlets. Cooperative Extension Service, Kansas State University, Manhattan, Ks. Many similar publications on vegetables and their diseases and pests are available from local or state extension services.

Plant Science (textbook, 674 pages). 1988. Prentice Hall, Englewood Cliffs, N.J. Reference information on growing plants.

Rodale's Color Handbook of Garden Insects (book, 243 pages). 1979. Rodale Press, Emmaus, Pa. Excellent color pictures and information on garden insects.

Rodale's Garden Problem Solver (book, 550 pages). 1988. Rodale Press, Emmaus, Pa. Good disease and pest control information (although grasshoppers are not in the index).

Index

Asparagus, 61
  growing essentials, 61
  pests and diseases, 64
  storing, 64
  varieties, 64

Bacillus popilliae, 35

Bacillus thuringiensis. See Bt

Beans, 64
  growing essentials, 65
  pests and diseases, 66
  storing, 66
  varieties, 66

Bees, 29, 92

Beets, 67
  growing essentials, 67
  pests and diseases, 70
  storing, 70
  varieties, 70

Beneficial insects, 28

Bermuda grass, 46

Biological pest controls, 35

Bindweed, 4, 46

Blackberries. *See* Huckleberries

Blanching vegetables for freezer storage, 66

Bolting, 96

Bordeaux mixture, 34

Broccoli, 70
  growing essentials, 71
  pests and diseases, 72
  storing, 74
  varieties, 74

Brussels sprouts, 73
  growing essentials, 73
  pests and diseases, 74
  storing, 74
  varieties, 74

Bt, 35

Cabbage, 74
  growing essentials, 74
  pests and diseases, 75
  storing, 75
  varieties, 75

Cantaloupe, 77
  growing essentials, 77
  pests and diseases, 78

storing, 79
  varieties, 79

Carrots, 79
  growing essentials, 79
  pests and diseases, 82
  storing, 82
  varieties, 82

Cauliflower, 75
  growing essentials, 76
  pests and diseases, 76
  varieties, 76

Celery, 83
  growing essentials, 83
  pests and diseases, 84
  storing, 84
  varieties, 84

Chives. *See* Onion family

Companion planting, 26

Compost, 4, 20

Corn, 84
  growing essentials, 85
  pests and diseases, 86
  storing, 87
  varieties, 87

Cucumbers, 87
  growing essentials, 88
  pests and diseases, 89
  storing, 90
  varieties, 90

Dill, 83
  growing essentials, 83
  pests and diseases, 84
  storing, 84
  varieties, 84

Disease
  anthracnose, 34, 42
  bacterial scab, 42
  blight, 34, 40
  damping off, 42
  fusarium, 40
  key to types on
    vegetables, 36
  leaf spot, 34, 40
  mildew, 34, 40
  mosaic virus, 42
  smut, 42
  stalk rot, 42
  wilts, 122

Drainage, 3, 6

Drip irrigation, 48

Eggplant, 90
  growing essentials, 91
  pests and diseases, 91
  storing, 91
  varieties, 94

Farmers' market, 59

Fertilizers, 18
  effects on soil pH, 21
  formulas on bags or
    containers, 18
  guide for using with each
    vegetable, 19
  liquid type for transplanting, 16

Fleeces, 26

Floating row covers, 23, 53

Flowers, 92, 137

Frost
  last killing in spring, 55
  first killing in fall, 56

Frost protection for transplants, 16

Fungicide
  synthetic, 36

Garden
  adding organic matter to,
    4
  choosing a location for,
    1
  drawing map of, 8
  fertilizing, 4
  making raised beds in, 5
  preparing new plot in, 3
  publications on, 1, 139
  testing the soil in, 4
  tilling, 4, 5
  using recommended-
    varieties lists for planting in, 9

Garlic. *See* Onion family

Grass clippings, 4

Gypsum, 4

Hail
  guide to treatment of
    hail-damaged plants,
    58
  ways to recover hail-

damaged garden, 54

Hairs, 68

Hotkaps, 16, 51

Hoses (soaker), 48, 53

Huckleberries, 94
  growing essentials, 94
  pests and diseases, 94
  storing, 94

Insecticidal soaps, 34

Insects, 25. *See also* Beneficial insects; Pests

Integrated pest management (IPM), 27

Lacewings, 29

Ladybugs, 28

Leafy greens, 95
  growing essentials, 95
  pests and diseases, 96
  storing, 96

Leaves, 4, 20

Lettuce
  varieties, 98

Lettuce (head)
  growing essentials, 97
  pests and diseases, 97
  storing, 98

Lettuce (leaf), 95. *See also* Leafy greens

Lime, 21

Manure, 4, 20

Mineral availability and pH, 21

Mulches, 22
  disposal of, 24
  getting an early start by using, 23
  pest control and, 24
  pest problems and, 24
  plastic, 23
  and soil temperature, 22
  types of, 22
  warming or cooling of soil with, 22
  and water conservation, 48, 53
  weed control and, 24

Netting, 39

Nitrogen, 18

Nosema locustae, 35

Nutrients, 18. *See also* Fertilizers

Okra, 99
  growing essentials, 99
  pests and diseases, 100
  storing, 100

varieties, 100

Onion family, 100
  growing essentials, 100
  pests and diseases, 101
  storing, 103
  varieties of, 103

Organic matter, 4, 21. *See also* Fertilizers

Parsley, 83
  growing essentials, 84
  pests and diseases, 84
  storing, 84
  varieties, 84

Peanuts, 103
  growing essentials, 103
  pests and diseases, 104
  storing, 104
  varieties, 104

Peas, 104
  growing essentials, 105
  pests and diseases, 105
  storing, 105
  varieties, 106

Peat moss, 4

Peppers, 106
  growing essentials, 107
  pests and diseases, 107
  storing, 108
  varieties, 108

Pests
  aphid, 34, 40
  asparagus beetle, 25, 34, 40
  bean leaf beetle, 25
  birds, 39
  cabbage worm, 25
  carrot weevil, 42
  Colorado potato beetle, 25, 34, 40
  corn earworm, 35, 40
  cricket, 40
  cucumber beetle, 26, 34
  cutworm, 25, 40
  deer, 38
  flea beetle, 27, 34, 40
  fruitworm, 40
  grasshopper, 25, 34, 35, 40
  hornworm, 35, 40
  June beetle grub, 40
  key to damage caused by, 36
  leaf-hopper, 26, 34, 42
  leaf-roller worm, 40
  looper, 34, 40
  Mexican bean beetle, 26, 34, 40
  mite, 34, 40
  onion maggot, 42
  parsley worm, 40
  pill bug (roly-polies), 34, 40

psyllids, 40, 110
  rabbit, 39
  raccoon, 39
  red spider, 40
  rhubarb cucurlio, 40
  slug, 40
  snail, 40
  squash bug, 27, 31, 34, 40
  thrip, 34, 40
  vine borer, 27, 34
  weevil, 27, 34, 40
  white grub, 35
  whitefly, 34, 40
  wireworm, 42
  worm, 35, 40

Pest and disease control, 25
  biological-mechanical, 25
  natural pesticides and fungicides, 33
  synthetic pesticides and fungicides, 35

Pesticides, 25
  to control grasshoppers, 35
  safety when using, 32
  synthetic, 35
  types of, 27, 36

pH, 20

Phloem, 122

Phosphorus, 18

Photosynthesis, 113, 122

Physiological problems
  blossom-end rot, 42
  cracking of cabbage heads, 42
  cracking of tomatoes, 42, 129
  leaf curl, 40
  tip burn, 40

Pollen, 80, 92

Pollination, 80, 92
  bees and, 92
  hand pollination of squash, 80
  insecticides and, 80

Potassium, 19, 113

Potatoes, 108
  growing essentials, 109
  pests and diseases, 110
  storing, 110
  varieties, 111

Praying mantises, 29

Pumpkins, 111
  growing essentials, 111
  pests and diseases, 115
  storing, 115
  varieties, 115

Pyrethrum, 34

Quackgrass, 46

Radishes, 112
  growing essentials, 114
  pests and diseases, 115
  storing, 115
  varieties, 115

Raised beds, 5, 48

Recipes, 131

Record keeping
  after a hailstorm, 57
  of successful vegetable
    varieties, 9

Rhizome, 46

Rhubarb, 115
  growing essentials, 116
  pests and diseases, 117
  storing, 117
  varieties, 117

Rotenone, 33

Roundup, 4

Sabadilla, 34

Scallions, 100

Scanning electron micro-
graph (SEM)
  bee and wasp stingers,
    102
  bee with pollen, 92
  orange-collared moth
    wing, 31
  plant hairs, 68
  pollen, 80
  praying mantis, 30
  soils, 6
  squash bug egg, 31
  stomata, 113
  transport system cells,
    122

Shallot. See Onion family

Soil, 6
  clay, 6
  drainage, 6
  improving by adding
    organic matter, 6
  pH, 20
  sandy, 7
  temperature of, 23

Spiders, 29

Spinach
  varieties of, 98
  See also Leafy greens

Squash, 117
  growing essentials, 118
  pests and diseases, 119
  pollinating by hand to set
    fruit, 80
  storing summer types,
    119
  storing winter types, 119

varieties, 119

Stomata, 68, 113

Straw, 4

Strawberries, 120
  growing essentials, 120
  pests and diseases, 124
  storing, 124
  varieties, 124

Succession planting, 8

Sulfur, 34

Sunlight, 2

Swartzberries, 94

Sweet potatoes, 125
  growing essentials, 125
  pests and diseases, 126
  storing, 126
  varieties, 126

Swiss chard
  varieties, 98
  See also Leafy greens

Thinning, 96
  beets, 67
  carrots, 82
  corn, 86
  leafy greens, 96
  radishes, 114

Tilling the soil, 4, 5

Tomatoes, 126
  cages for growing in
    wind-prone areas, 51
  cracking, 129
  growing essentials, 127
  methods for ripening,
    129
  pests and diseases, 129
  storing, 129
  varieties, 130

Transpiration, 113

Transplanting, 16
  fertilizer and, 16
  hotkap and, 16
  Wallo'Water and, 16

Transplants
  advantages of, 10
  cost of, 11
  fertilizing of, 14
  growing, 14
  hardening, 15
  light for germinating, 14
  light for growing, 14
  materials needed for, 11
  temperatures for grow-
    ing, 14
  trays, 12

Transport systems
  sugars and, 122
  water and minerals and,
    122

Trellises, 52

Vegetables
  guide to symptoms and
    treatments of prob-
    lems for, 40
  importance of variety
    selection of, 5
  key to pest, disease, and
    physiological problems
    for, 36
  wind-resistant varieties
    of, 52.
  See also individual variet-
    ies

Wallo'Water
  energy capture and
    release with, 17
  hardening of transplants
    in, 15
  for protecting transplants
    from wind, frost,
    freeze, hail, and snow,
    with, 17, 51
  starting plants extra early
    in the garden with, 17,
    60
  with cucumbers for early
    start, 89
  with peppers, 107
  with tomatoes for early
    start, 128
  warming of soil with, 128

Wasps, 29, 102

Watering, 47, 52
  best time of day for, 48
  deep soaking, 48, 122
  drip irrigation, 48
  mulches, 48
  overhead sprinkling, 48,
    68, 113
  soaker hoses, 48

Watermelon, 77
  growing essentials, 77
  pests and diseases, 78
  storing, 79
  varieties, 79

Weed control, 24, 44

Weeds, 44

Wind, 50
  methods for preventing
    damage to plants by,
    51

Windbreaks, 48, 52

Xylem, 122